REDISCOVERING A PEARL OF GREAT PRICE

The Surprising Sacrament of Matrimony

Rev. Thomas L. Vandenberg

REDISCOVERING A PEARL OF GREAT PRICE
The Surprising Sacrament of Matrimony
Copyright © 2012 by Rev. Thomas L. Vandenberg
All rights reserved.

Published with ecclesiastical approval.

ISBN - 13:978-146 8089899

ISBN - 10 146808 9897

Dedicated to my parents,
Albert and Joyce Vandenberg.
It all began with them.

TABLE OF CONTENTS

Acknowledgements

Introduction   1

Chapter One: A Vocation to Remember   11
 "Honey, guess who called today."

Chapter Two: A Matrimonial Spirituality   27
 "What did "He" want?"

Chapter Three: Entering the Mystery   39
 "We're invited to a dance."

Chapter Four: Love Me, Love Me Not   49
 "Honey, we need to talk."

Chapter Five: The Depth and Breadth of Love   65
 "God wants us to be dance instructors."

Chapter Six: A Prophetic Voice   77
 "Are you sure it wasn't a wrong number?"

Chapter Seven: Bearers of Hope   97
 "But you know how I step on toes."

Chapter Eight: A Call to Unity   125
 "You mean I have to dance with everyone?"

Chapter Nine: Little Things Mean a Lot   145
 "Not to worry."

Appendix A: Pastoral Concerns
 1. Contraception   171

 2. Same Sex Marriage   179

 3. Cohabitation   190

Appendix B: Poems   195

ACKNOWLEDGEMENTS

There is no way to acknowledge all the people who had a hand in the development of this book, especially those married couples who have been a part of my life, beginning with my parents. In so many ways, I saw a goodness in them that was truly extraordinary, although it wore the mask of the ordinary most of the time. In time, I gradually discovered the truth that their goodness came from their commitment to love no matter what, that they were responding to the grace of God at work in their lives. I thank them all, even the ones who have long gone to their eternal reward. I also thank those who heard me speak and reassured me that I was onto something worthwhile and who encouraged me to write my thoughts down in book form. Encouragement came also from brother priests in my Jesus Caritas Fraternity, especially Father Mike McDermott. I thank those who helped edit the text, kept me on focus, and who guided me through some difficult areas: among them being Ralph Horner, Robin LaMoria, Pat and Gretchen McCarthy, Joe McQuiston, Tracey Rockwell, and David Thomas, PhD. of the Bethany Family Institute. And a special thanks to Mary Walton who did all the technical stuff. But above all, I am grateful to a gracious God who created us in the divine likeness, a likeness that has to include a sense of humor. After all, God did create us male and female. Now, if that isn't proof of a divine sense of humor, I don't know what is.

INTRODUCTION

A couple had just gone to bed when they hear a strange noise coming from downstairs. *"Do you hear that?"* the husband asked. *"Yes,"* said his wife with a bit of fear in her voice. So they both get up and go to see what's up. Sure enough, they catch a burglar in the act of stealing their silver. Caught red-handed, the burglar turns to them and says sternly, *"This means I have to kill you."* So he draws a gun and aims it at the wife, but just before pulling the trigger he pauses and asks her in a demanding voice, *"What's your name?"* Now trembling, she answers meekly, *"Elizabeth."* *"Elizabeth!"* the man says with unexpected respect in his voice. *"That's my mother's name. I can't shoot you."* So he aims the gun at the husband and asks, *"What's your name?"* The husband answers, *"My name is Jack . . . but everybody calls me Elizabeth."*

From this little story we see that the way we look at things makes all the difference. The popular lecturer, Wayne Dyer, often seen on Public Television, says that when we change the way we look at things, the things we look at change. This book is about changing the way we look at marriage, especially the Sacrament of Matrimony. While both are sacred unions, marriage and the Sacrament of Matrimony are not synonyms. And we need to stop looking at them as if they were.

I can't help but think of the observation attributed to Michelangelo when he said the problem isn't that we set goals so high we can't reach them, but rather that we set them so low we can. It seems to me that for years we have been "dumbing down" our understanding of marriage. It is little wonder that many in our society, including some Catholics, now regard marriage as only a legal document hardly worth the paper it is written on. And, ironically, at the very same time, many of our brothers and sisters in the gay community want to redefine marriage and are willing to do almost anything to get their relationship certified as a true marriage. It appears that the significance of marriage has been so compromised that it can apply to any relationship as long as the two parties are committed to each other in love . . . or something like that.

Although I knew something was off key about this view of marriage, I could have succumbed to it myself if it hadn't been for the influence of some wonderful people in my life, especially married couples. My objective is not to get embroiled in this controversy, although it cannot be totally ignored. It is to show the effects of my gradual rediscovery of the Sacrament of Matrimony as a way of life that, when lived fully, has such surprising characteristics that it will both challenge and bring out the best of those who enter it. I began to see it as such a "pearl of great price" that I think people will not be so inclined to take it for granted or demand that they have a right to receive it. It is a vocation, a call from God if you will, that can best be seen as a gift. I honestly believe that many couples who do not regard marriage as a sacrament may come to look at sacramental couples as models of how they would like to live out their commitment of married love. It is a way of life that demands the best of who they are as human beings and as followers of Jesus, rather than a simple, legal, living arrangement with public approval that demands nothing.

And yet, to my surprise, no one seems to be addressing the significance of, or the practical meaning of the Sacrament of Matrimony. Really, do you know anyone who can tell you the difference between sacramental and non-sacramental marriage? Okay, canonists tell us a sacramental marriage requires two baptized people. That's right, but it doesn't reveal what the sacramental part actually means. What difference does it make if someone is baptized or not? What is it about those baptisms that make a marriage a sacrament? Or better yet, what is "sacramental" about it? These are not just academic questions, but questions that need answering if our couples are ever to discover their vital role in the church as sacramental couples. While I've tried to write this book in a style that can be easily understood by ordinary people with a limited theological vocabulary, I also wanted to speak to both priests and bishops at the same time. This is a serious book with serious implications for both our couples and the church. My seemingly quirky use of humor in unexpected places is not just for the reader's enjoyment but also to help make the point I'm trying to get across.

In all honesty, I am surprised that someone hasn't written this book already. Certainly there are many who know theology much better than I, particularly the theology of matrimony from a Roman Catholic perspective. I would love to be a scholar, but when our Lord was passing out talents, that isn't one I was given. I must say, there are few people in the church that I have as much respect for as those theologians who have devoted their lives to learning and teaching the wonderful truths of faith; who know the history of doctrinal development and its scriptural and traditional underpinnings; who open for us the riches of new understanding. In more ways than one, we would truly be lost without them. But, apparently, none of them thought of writing this book.

Next to these scholars are those men and women whose wonderful insights can take complex theology and translate it into a simpler language for people like me. Some are scholars in their own right, like Catherine LaCugna and Sister Elizabeth Johnson. I've seldom ever rubbed shoulders with any top scholar, although one time I was asked to drive the late Raymond Brown, S.S. to the airport after he gave a seminar to the priests of the Archdiocese of Seattle. What an opportunity to learn one-on-one from one of the world's finest scripture scholars. But as we drove along, all he seemed interested in was my world, especially beautiful Mt. Rainier which loomed in the distance over the Kent valley like a huge ice cream sundae. I still smile when I recall that day.

I think of the hours I've spent listening to tapes and CD's by people like Fr. Richard Rohr, O.F.M. from the Center of Action and Contemplation in Albuquerque and Fr. Michael Himes from Boston College. They have a way of revealing the riches of profound truths in simple ways, and of opening avenues of understanding for people who have neither the time nor opportunity, not to mention the interest, to do the "heavy lifting" themselves. While they could have written this book, they didn't.

And I would also be remiss if I didn't acknowledge the many scholarly writers in the Catholic press who have fed me over the years, as well as those learned men and women whom I turn to daily for ideas for preaching, like the contributors to the **Weekday Homily Helps** from St. Anthony Messenger Press. Those who live in the academic world may recognize names like Norman Langenbrunner, Barbara Leonard, O.S.F., Mary Ann Getty or J. Patrick Mullen, but to me they are just people who have bailed me out of a tough spot or sparked an idea that worked its way into a homily some cold winter morning. Actually, I did meet Father Mullen. He is a seminary professor of sacred scripture. They may not be the "big hitters" we've heard about, but they are more than qualified to play the game very well at the "Triple A" level. They are my heroes, and maybe someday, their names will be familiar to the ordinary fans of the church. Over the years, they have nourished me in countless ways. Many of the ideas in this book came from them, although I can't remember exactly which article or commentary they were in. In other words, when I think I'm having an original thought, it was probably planted in my head by someone else. But again, that someone else didn't write them down in the book form we created here.

Actually, when I think of it, the ones most qualified to write this book are married couples themselves. They could have written much of it from firsthand experience. I would imagine that as they read these pages they will come across things that trigger a distant memory or spark one of those "aha" moments. Some may ask, *"Why didn't I think of that?"* When they do hear something totally new, it is probably because they just never thought of things quite the way I do. But they will be able to accept what is said because it is totally compatible with their experience as married couples and people of faith.

We can't ignore the importance of the married couples in our lives. As I recall the story, shortly after his ordination as a bishop, Pope John XXIII reportedly showed his new Episcopal ring to his mother. She looked at it, then showed him her wedding ring and said, *"You wouldn't be wearing that ring if I wasn't wearing this one."* We can't sell short the impact of the Catholic atmosphere in our homes as we grew up, mostly created by our parents. We breathed it in and breathed it out day after day as part of the maturing process. My guess is that our parents were so close to the subtly of it all that they couldn't see it themselves. Maybe they were just too busy trying to raise us, and that is why they didn't write this book.

In a certain sense, then, it is almost by default that I write about my own personal discovery of the importance of the Sacrament of Matrimony. Over the years it became clearer and clearer to me that some things needed to be said about marriage in the Catholic Church that were just not being said. If they are now, I am not hearing them. I listened to a bishop speak at length on the state of marriage in the Catholic Church and he never once mentioned that it was a sacrament. While it was an interesting talk, what he said could have been said about any marriage, religious or not. The uniqueness of sacramental marriage as understood in the Catholic Church was simply passed over. I can't imagine a bishop talking about the priestly ministry without at least alluding somewhere along the way to the Sacrament of Orders as a unique vocation from God. In addition, I've looked over the list of presentations the past few years of a major catechetical congress for a talk on the Sacrament of Matrimony. There hasn't been any. Why? It seems that this wonderful sacrament of the Church is sailing along under the radar when it should be held up for the world to see. Something has to change! And that is one big reason why I wrote this book.

But there are other reasons, too. One day it dawned on me that Robert Fulghum was wrong. While his book **All I Really Need to Know I Learned in Kindergarten** may be a very good and a truly helpful book, a kindergarten cannot replace a loving home and the atmosphere of faithful love that is in the air that everyone breathes. And that atmosphere is created primarily by husbands and wives in their day in and day out efforts to love each other and their families. They witness to a committed love that does not end when it's 4 o'clock in the afternoon. In a home, there is no such thing as "after hours." It is a couple's committed love that not only conceived their children, but it is their committed love that continues the creation of their children so they will grow up to be healthy human beings. While it is important to support kindergarten teachers, it is far more important that we give real support and encouragement to mothers and fathers as husbands and wives. After all, we as a church are very explicit in saying that parents are the primary educators of their children. Our married couples deserve to know we are in their corner, helping and cheering them on. That's another reason I wrote this book.

But there are more reasons still that I became aware of, and some are quite surprising. It seems that the church just assumes that the Sacrament of Matrimony is a "needy sacrament," that is to say, those who enter this state in life always need to be ministered to. Married couples always seem to be seen as on the receiving end of ministry. Somewhere along the way many of us priests decided, because we were priests I suppose, that we were the ones to give that help. After all, aside from some class in college or a brief pre-Cana effort in the local parish before their wedding, few couples ever studied any real theology about marriage like we priests had. And we celibate priests have read all kinds of things about love and stuff like that. Of course they need us to show them what married love is all about. Maybe, but not so fast.

Granted, there are times when we priests are truly helpful to our couples. But very often, our couples have much to teach us priests. You'd be surprised at the number of times I have overheard couples speak lovingly of their pastors, hoping against hope that they would "get out of their heads," stop being so aloof, and not be so defensive of their authority; some bishops, too. Their words were never spoken in a condescending manner because they truly loved, respected and believed in their priests and bishops. As you will see in this book, our couples are truly the ones who are the experts on relationships and what makes them work. And they have so much to teach us about relationships, about life, about the Church, and, may I add, even about the priesthood.

Since my ordination to the priesthood in 1962, I have personally found a high level of comfort being with married couples. While I was always close to my family and regularly spend my day off with my brother priests, I most often spent much of my other down time with married couples and their families. Over the years, I have been attracted especially to couples who clearly loved each other, who were close to the church, and who had a real respect for the priesthood. It was important for me to be a friend to both the husband and wife. I had no idea that I was actually in a unique classroom of learning; but now, years later, I look back and see the many things I learned just from watching, listening and being there.

Then, in the early 70's, I got involved with Worldwide Marriage Encounter and soon found myself working with married couples. That is when my real awakening, my real education blossomed, not just about marriage but also about priesthood and about the church and about life. It was then that my understanding of the theology of the Sacrament of Matrimony began to evolve. Among my mentors were the many couples I worked with, like Pete and Nancy Wright of Seattle, Al and Barbara Reigner of California and priests in leadership roles, especially Father Charles A. Gallagher, S.J. of New York, as well as the good, ordinary couples making the WWME weekend who shared their stories. But there are countless more couples who never made a weekend that I have learned much from as well. The fingerprints of all these couples are on every page of this book.

Providentially, in 1983 I was assigned to St. Vincent de Paul Parish in Federal Way, Washington, a parish that had a tradition of supporting marriage and family life. It had a Family Ministry Office and a full time paid staff person in place. Among other things, I inherited an Annual Lovers' Celebration near Valentine's Day that we kept alive even after such celebrations were no longer "in." In time, the parish embraced new ministries to support married couples even more. For stay-at-home moms, it was Mothers and Others and one we simply called a *"Couples' Night Out."* I was asked to write some talks on marriage to support our couples. Then, thanks to the help from a neighboring parish, the Marriage Renewal Weekend began in 2002. I couldn't get away from married couples even if I tried!

While all this was going on, I continued to watch and listen and learn. Pretty soon, I was asked to share my thoughts on the Sacrament of Matrimony in other parishes, which I was happy to do. I remember one woman telling me after hearing my vision for marriage in the church, *"I wish I had heard that when I was raising my kids. I had no support and never felt so alone."* I have also shared my ideas on sacramental marriage with priests and permanent deacon candidates with their wives. I even gave a retreat for married couples with a bishop present the whole time. His support reinforced my belief that I was on to something important that needed to be said. As mentioned, some encouraged me to put my thoughts in book form. Apparently, my remarks were striking a chord. And it became even clearer to me that no one else was going to say it, so I was going to have to say it myself.

Consequently, that's how I came to write this book. I hope that married couples who read it will come away with an awareness of the importance of their love for each other and the special role they have as a married couple in the life of the Church, a role that is fundamental to the kind of church we become in the world. And should the engaged or even pre-engaged young people read it, I hope they will become excited about how God may be calling them to such a lofty vocation so they will prepare for it accordingly. I am hopeful that the ideas presented here will help my brother priests in their important ministries to and with married couples. It would be wonderful if a bishop or two were to acquire a renewed vision of this important sacrament and its significance for the renewal of the church in their dioceses.

When I was in the seminary, every Wednesday seminarians would visit patients in nearby hospitals and nursing homes. The story is told that after one such day, a returning seminarian reported his experience with a woman who had asked him for his priestly blessing. He said to her, *"I'm not a priest yet,"* and refused to bless her. Unfazed, she asked again, *"Oh Father, your blessing is important to me. Please."* He said to her, *"I can't. I'm only a seminarian. I'm not ordained."* But she persisted, *"It would mean everything to me, Father. Please."* Realizing he was getting nowhere, he said over her while tracing the Sign of the Cross, *"Nemo dat quod non habet; In nomine Patris, et Filii et Spiritus Sancti. Amen."* She smiled and thanked him profusely. What he had said was, *"I can't give what I don't have; In the name of the Father and of the Son and of the Holy Spirit. Amen."* (Be careful. Latin only sounds holy.)

I can't give what I don't have, either. But what I do have needs to be said. So, let's begin now to take a good look at the surprising Sacrament of Matrimony. If we change the way we look at it, it will change. May the rediscovery begin!

CHAPTER ONE

A VOCATION TO REMEMBER

"Honey, guess who called today."

A man and a woman are standing at the altar about to be married when the bride-to-be notices a set of golf clubs the groom had placed near the sacristy door. She looked at him and whispered, *"What on earth are those golf clubs doing here?"* He responded, *"This isn't going to take all afternoon is it?"*

Let me begin by saying that I believe the Sacrament of Matrimony is the most neglected, if not abused sacrament in the Catholic Church. I realize that this is a pretty harsh statement, but it's the way I see it. I hope it got your attention. My reasons for saying this will become evident as we go along. Let's begin with this observation. When two Catholics want to marry, the Catholic Church legislates that the wedding must take place according to church law. I have no problem with this. But the law makes getting married in the church so important that, should that couple choose to marry "outside the church," a penalty will be imposed upon them for doing so. If Catholics do not profess their vows before a properly delegated Catholic priest or a Catholic deacon and two witnesses, and if there is no proper dispensation from this sacramental form, they will be considered to be living in sin and will not be allowed to receive Holy Communion until the marriage is "blessed." While such persons are not formally excommunicated for marrying outside of the church, it is easy to understand why many think they are.

That couple may wonder why what they did is seen as so wrong that they can no longer participate fully in the Mass by receiving Holy Communion. They still love God, go to Mass, want their babies baptized and some even want to come to confession. But sadly, an answer is seldom given them other than to say they broke church law. And since they are technically living in sin . . . well, you know the rest. It is seldom made clear why the Catholic Church takes this sacrament so seriously. Now, while there is no doubt a good explanation for this ecclesial legislation, in the minds of the ordinary lay person it is simply seen as a punishment for not obeying the rules (canon law). The theology behind the law is rarely explained. The guilty parties are left wondering why there are such dire consequences for not having their wedding in the Church.

There is no ecclesial penalty if they don't get confirmed or anointed when sick. And should they commit some sin that excludes them from receiving Holy Communion, they can go to confession and that pretty much takes care of it. But withholding the Eucharist from those who marry outside the church, not to mention that their marriage isn't even recognized as valid by the Church is pretty stiff. To be reinstated as practicing Catholics, they must choose between separating from one another, living as brother and sister or having their marriage validated by the Church. Unfortunately, in this day and age, just telling people they have to do something under penalty of sin doesn't cut it. They want to know the reasons, and the reasons had better make sense.

Many priests have shared with me that the number of weddings they are celebrating in their parishes has dropped off considerably. Mary Beth Celio, Director of Research for the Archdiocese of Seattle, confirms this observation. Using data from **The Official Catholic Directory of the United States** from 1991 to 2008, she shows that there is a 45% drop in the number of weddings being celebrated in the Catholic Church nationally. While there may be many factors that go into this startling drop off, from a lack of faith commitment to cultural pressures, the burden of guilt does not just rest there. From my experience, the church does not go out of its way to encourage or to invite its young couples to receive the Sacrament of Matrimony, let alone explain why they should. In most cases, priests simply wait for engaged couples to come to the church to get married, doing little to reach out to them.

For example, at our Annual Youth Convention for teens, I have observed that there is always a workshop on vocations to the priesthood and religious life, but there is never anything about marriage, specifically, the Sacrament of Matrimony. For the life of me, I can't figure out why. Maybe the planners think that teens are too young to be exposed to this sacrament for fear it might encourage them to get married too young. Should that be true, can't that same argument be applied to the common practice of recruiting teens to consider the priesthood and religious life? Many dioceses have a program called *"Quo Vadis"* designed specifically for young men from 13 to 18 years of age to encourage them to consider a possible vocation to the priesthood. Why aren't they considered too young also? God forbid that anyone thinks getting married, even in the church, just isn't considered religious enough to merit a place on the agenda. It's a sacrament for heaven's sake!

It is often said that a church budget is really a theological statement. It reveals the values of those who make it up; it's a statement of priorities. I would venture to say that in the vast majority of dioceses in our country, there is considerable funding for Marriage Tribunals to help couples get out of one marriage so they can enter another marriage in the Church. I have no argument with this. But there is virtually nothing reflected in their budgets to help encourage and prepare couples or to assist parishes in encouraging and preparing couples to enter the vocation of sacramental marriage in the first place. Now, that does bother me.

Almost every diocese has a vocation director, but, again, only for the priesthood and religious life. They spend virtually no time, energy or funds to reach out to young people to encourage them to enter the Sacrament of Matrimony. Until each diocese has a vocations office that encourages and supports the Sacrament of Matrimony along with the Sacrament of Orders and religious life, I don't see how we can say we are taking seriously the whole notion of vocations in, of and for the church.

If vocations to priesthood and the religious life begin at home, as was the conventional wisdom when I was growing up, it seems to me that the importance of the home cannot be ignored in the "vocation hunt." Sadly, the situation has deteriorated to the point that in many homes the idea of priestly and religious vocations is outright discouraged. Remember the old story about the babies floating down the river, and people scurrying to rescue them? Finally, someone decided to go up the river to find out where the babies were coming from in the first place. Well, our situation is the reverse of that. To a great extent, ecclesial vocations have "dried up." We need to go up the river to find out why. We can't just stand around and wonder why our youth are not coming to us to become priests, religious or to get married.

We need to take the initiative. While I am no more in favor of *recruiting* kids to marriage than I am in favor of *recruiting* kids to the priesthood or religious life, I do believe it is important to plant seeds by heightening the awareness in our youth that matrimony is a sacred vocation to which God may eventually call them, not just the Sacrament of Orders or the consecrated life of a religious. We simply cannot allow the Sacrament of Matrimony to be seen as the default vocation meant to pop up on the screen of life when all else fails. It deserves better.

Another oft-missed opportunity to extend an invitation to the vocation of matrimony occurs during the celebration of the Sacrament of Confirmation. The bishop frequently works into his homily a few words to encourage vocations. That is good, especially since confirmation is the sacrament out of which our young people will live their faith in the future. But when the bishop talks about vocations, he, again, only mentions the priesthood and religious life. While the shortage of priests and religious is critical, the bishop never mentions the Sacrament of Matrimony as a vocation in, of and for the church for them to consider also. In reality, I believe there is a shortage of couples who truly value the Sacrament of Matrimony that is just as critical as the current shortage of priests and religious.

It's hard to imagine that any bishop might think that matrimony is somehow a threat to Holy Orders or the religious life. Sacred vocations, since they come from God, cannot be in competition, one against the other. When truly understood, they are complimentary. Just a few words of encouragement about the vocation of matrimony by the bishop at this most teachable moment could do wonders for those who will consider marriage in the future - like 99% of those sitting in front of him waiting to be confirmed.

* * * * * * *

I watched a young woman grow up in our parish. I really liked her spirit. She was bright, spunky and faithful. We would often just talk about stuff. She was involved in the youth program, came to Mass weekly, went through Confirmation, and then, about a year or so after graduation from high school, I learned that she had gotten married; not in the parish; not in the Catholic Church anywhere. I was shocked and wondered why she hadn't even come to talk to me about her proposed marriage. Apparently, getting married in the Catholic Church didn't register with her. It is as if she hadn't ever heard she needed to. And since she was my parishioner, I felt sad, even guilty because I figured that I shared some of the blame. There was a time when we could safely assume our young people would want to marry in the church, but we can't assume that any longer. And since the spirit in our culture says, *"No one is going to tell me what to do."* we need to find positive ways to show our young couples that getting married in the Catholic Church has something to offer them that they simply will not find anywhere else.

I recall an engaged couple in our marriage prep program that suddenly stopped coming to class. A few weeks later I saw them at Mass. *"Where have you been?"* I asked. *"Oh, we got married!"* *"Where?"* I asked in disbelief. *"By a judge,"* they said. *"But why?"* I persisted. *"Because we couldn't afford to get married in the church."* I told them that it didn't cost hardly anything to get married in our church. What costs big money are clothes, flowers, and receptions. The most important part of the wedding day, the ceremony, is virtually peanuts cost-wise. In their case, since they were parishioners and of little means, the cost would have been nothing.

(Sometimes I tell couples it costs 10% of whatever they are spending on clothes and flowers just to watch their faces drain of blood.) Apparently, this young couple had no idea the church had something to offer them that they couldn't get from the local judge. It is critical that we address just what that something is.

I occasionally hear priests say that the Catholic Church should get out of the marrying business. I can understand why, especially when a couple comes to the parish to get married with no commitment to the church, let alone to the Catholic Faith. Some say we should have two ceremonies, like in other countries. The civil ceremony takes care of the legal aspects of the marriage and the church ceremony takes care of the religious aspects of the marriage. I'm not sure how this helps because the church does not recognize the marriage until it is validated in the church anyway. But in America, the priest represents both the church and state. And in all truth, even in parishes with good marriage preparation programs, some couples are simply not ready to receive the Sacrament of Matrimony. Be that as it may, one thing is for sure: the couple is still bound and determined to get married . . . somewhere. For many, the church is just their preferred choice, but other options are often on the table. And since their marriages outside the church would not be recognized by the church as valid, priests and deacons often feel trapped to officiate at their weddings. In effect, they are functioning like they are just civil ministers, all religious trappings notwithstanding. Why not just let the civil authorities handle all weddings? (cf. Appendix A-3 on Cohabitation)

I have another take on this. I've never considered the church to be in the marrying business. As a church, we are about calling couples to a unique way of life. We Catholics can no more turn marriage over to the state to perform for us than we can ask the state to perform our baptisms. What would a couple think if their pastor told them to take their child to the courthouse to have it baptized? They'd be shocked and scandalized and go look for another priest. Of course, asking a civil official to baptize your child is ludicrous. Baptism is a sacrament. So, for a Catholic, why isn't getting married by a civil judge ludicrous? It is a sacrament, too! Like all sacraments, the Sacrament of Matrimony is part of the sacred treasury of the Church. Yet, our couples get married by judges, not to mention other religious ministers, all the time. Why? Well, there are a lot of reasons. But one major reason is that they have absolutely no idea what the Sacrament of Matrimony means. That is what I want to address. Our married couples need to know just how precious they are, even how crucial they are to the healthy life of the Church. As I've said, we are not in the marrying business. We are about calling people to a way of life in keeping with God's plan for the church.

* * * * * * *

Of course, most marriages in the world are not sacramental, yet they can be very rewarding and fulfilling relationships. In fact, these couples may well be fulfilling God's plan for them, that they are "two in one flesh." Their call is to unity and the fullness of life. They may be exactly like a sacramental marriage except for one thing, and that one thing is not God. God is present in Jewish marriages, Buddhist marriages and Muslim marriages, none of which is seen as sacramental. God is present in secular, even atheist marriages, but I don't tell them; it's too upsetting. You see, marriage, by its very nature, images God the creator whether the couple knows it or not or likes it or not. Of its nature it is generative. It gives life. Remember, the crown of creation was neither the creation of the man nor the creation of the woman. It was the creation of the man/woman. They are called to a unity of love, the image of God.

The one thing that distinguishes sacramental from non-sacramental marriage, the one thing that makes the Sacrament of Matrimony unique is the explicit covenant relationship that a married couple enters into on their wedding day. But it is not the covenant relationship they enter into with God, as that can be true of other believers of other faiths. Nor is it the covenant relationship the couple enter with each other, which is also a common belief of people of faith and other persons of good will. What makes the Sacrament of Matrimony unique is the covenant relationship the couple enters into with the other members of the church, the Body of Christ. That is the distinctive element of sacramental marriage.

Put it this way. Sacraments are not just for the persons receiving them. They are also for the life of the church. Baptism, Confirmation, Eucharist all help build, unify and strengthen the church, not just the people who receive them. The anointing of the sick not only brings God's healing grace to the infirm, it also brings consolation to their family members. But this is especially evident when we compare the Sacrament of Matrimony with the only other social sacrament of the church, Holy Orders. It is obvious that I am not a priest for me. I wish I could absolve myself from sin, but I can't. I can't anoint myself when I am sick, either. I am ordained for others. And those "others" are the people I am called to serve as a priest at any given time. When a couple gets married in the Catholic Church, assuming they are baptized, the sacrament they receive is not primarily for them. It is for us; it is above all for the life of the church. That is why, along with the Sacrament of Orders, it is called a social sacrament. I will expand on this a bit later, but for now, this needs to sink in. Surprise!

How many couples have any inkling of this when they exchange their vows in church? They think it is all about them. Contrast this with the ordination of a priest. He knows he is being ordained for others, not himself, and so does everyone who sees the bishop lay hands on his head. At a wedding, when the couple exchanges vows, the thought just doesn't cross anyone's mind. Yes, welcome to the first surprise of this wonderful gift to the church, the Sacrament of Matrimony.

Let me digress for a minute about canon law, which is the governing law of the Catholic Church, and how it impacts sacramental marriage. A few things need to be clear in our minds. To receive the sacraments of the church, a person must be baptized first. If a person is not baptized, he/she cannot receive the Sacrament of Matrimony. Canonically speaking, both husband and wife need to be baptized for a marriage to be regarded as a sacrament. Therefore, if one party is not baptized, the marriage is not sacramental; holy and sacred perhaps, but not sacramental. For such a marriage to be celebrated in the Catholic Church, a special dispensation is required by the church. But should the non-baptized person receive baptism at a later date, regardless of denomination, the marriage becomes sacramental at that moment, no further wedding ceremony is required. (Mormon baptisms are not accepted as valid sacraments by the Catholic Church.)

If one party is Catholic and the other is a baptized Protestant, the marriage is still considered sacramental. If two Protestants are baptized, their marriage is also seen as sacramental by the Catholic Church, but they don't really care what the Church says, unless, of course, they divorce and then one wants to marry a Catholic. A truly sacramental marriage is indissoluble, that is, it cannot be broken, while that may be possible for non-sacramental marriages under certain specific circumstances. Some apparently sacramental marriages may not be marriages at all, but I don't want to get into all of that. It can get pretty confusing. Besides, I think that's enough canon law for now.

To be quite frank here, I fear that canon law, as good, important and necessary as it is, a fact I don't question, has had something of a toxic effect on our appreciation of the Sacrament of Matrimony. The law has virtually taken over our understanding of what makes a sacramental marriage sacramental in practice, as though it were only a legal entity. As I recall when we studied marriage in the seminary, the course was pretty much all about canon law. The minimal theology of marriage we did get was almost an afterthought. (I can only hope things are better now.) Unfortunately, canon law has the potential of being so dehumanizing to sacramental marriage that the sacramental part can be virtually stripped of practical meaning, its efficacy totally ignored. Sadly, I know Catholics whose marriages are canonically sacramental, but are neither generative nor life-giving and have nothing to do with a life of faith.

I overheard a young priest say he wanted to study canon law so he could learn more about the Sacrament of Matrimony. I shook my head at his lack of understanding. The laws surrounding the sacrament are not the same as the sacrament. Again, I am not being critical of canon law. It serves a very important role in the orderly life of the church and cannot be ignored. But by itself, it is not enough if we want to understand the importance of the Sacrament of Matrimony. It would be like sending someone to study the beauty of Mozart's music and just have him learn the rules of harmony and composition that Mozart used. Like Mozart's music, matrimony is something that embodies the human spirit and expresses it in infinite ways. It is meant to inspire and give life, to comfort and to be absorbed. It is meant to go beyond itself to touch the hearts of others and enhance the experience of human existence.

Besides, the Sacrament of Matrimony existed long before the canon law of marriage was ever written. Canon law does not and cannot call us to a way of life! If we just look at matrimony from a legalistic point of view, there won't be much that is attractive about it. It will be stripped of its power to inspire and give life. As a canon lawyer once said at a gathering of us priests, *"Treat canon law as you would a bed pan. Keep it discretely out of sight until you need it."* I've always taken that as good advice.

Matrimony is a call, a vocation, from God through the Church that asks a couple, *"Will you spend your love of each other for us?"* *"Will you allow us to look to you as a sign of how we are to love one another in the Church?"* *"Will you allow us to continue to call you to live your life of unity and love more totally as time goes by . . . even at those times when you do not feel like loving each other?"* Parishioners want their priest, as a priest, to spend his life for them. Right? After all, that is a priest's call from God and the Church. We understand that. If his behavior becomes a scandal to the church, his people can call the bishop to do something about it. Why can't we priests, in the name of all of God's People, ask our married couples, call them, invite them, encourage them to spend their love for us? It's not just between the couple. When they marry in the Catholic Church, they let the People of God in on their love. We might say that the marriage is for the couple; the sacrament is for us. In other words, the sacrament calls the married couple to a breadth of love, even if it isn't foremost on their minds at the beginning.

* * * * * * *

Clearly, there must be something very special about a married couple's love for each other that the church came to recognize centuries ago; something so special that nobody else has it in such a clear and life-giving way; something so special that the church saw it as sacramental. What is it? When a husband and wife are both living out the call of their baptism, they become a living sign, not only of God the creator, as is true of all married couples, but also a living sign of Jesus the redeemer. In fact, it's even more than that. They are more than examples of, or models of Jesus' love. As a Sacrament, they bring something of Jesus' love into our lives. Their presence among us, within our community, is a grace. In an exceptionally powerful way, they make Jesus' love real in our world. So much so, that I personally believe that our sacramental couples deserve to be honored, even reverenced, as much as any person ordained to the Sacrament of Orders.

Our couples deserve to be believed in as much as we believe in the Sacrament of Baptism or the Real Presence of Jesus in the Eucharist. You see, being believed in is crucial, for when someone believes in us, we are empowered. I often ask couples coming to get married how they felt when they realized their sweetheart believed in them. They always say something like, *"I felt valued, joyful and important; like a king/queen. I felt empowered."* Conversely, according to St. Mark's account of the Gospel, Jesus could perform no miracles in Nazareth because of the peoples' lack of faith in him *(Mk 6:4-6)*. Being believed in empowers us.

Well, in the Sacrament of Matrimony, the Church is technically making an act of faith in our sacramental couples, which should empower them to realize that they are unique and special in the eyes of the faithful, the church, including their priests and bishops, not to mention God. However, we must find ways to make that act of faith more than something technical. It must become something tangible, explicit and real, that our couples can sense is always there for them, and not just on their wedding day.

Very often couples will think their vocation is to be parents. Not quite! They didn't receive the sacrament of parenthood. They received the Sacrament of Matrimony. Parenthood is a grace of matrimony. They didn't get married just to have kids. They got married to love each other, and in the context of their love for each other, they had kids. As you should have heard many times, the greatest gift a husband can give his children is to love their mother, and the greatest gift a mother can give her children is to love their father. That is what will keep the proper balance in the family and make the home environment secure. That is what will free the children from their primary fear, which is to be abandoned by one of their parents. Why do they fear that? Because that is what happened to so many of their friends at school.

At the height of the cold war, I recall a television movie called **The Morning After** which received a great deal of media hype. The publicity and anticipation of the movie became intense as it depicted the devastation caused by nuclear warheads that were delivered by Soviet missiles that struck the USA. A local school district did a survey of its children about their fears, as the hype grew more passionate as the airing of the movie neared. The results were telling. As it turned out, their #1 fear was not nuclear war, which was way down the list, but the fear of being abandoned by one of their parents.

I'll never forget the woman who told me that when she was eight years old her parents divorced. *"At night,"* she said, *"I'd go into my mother's bedroom to see if she was still there."* Many years ago, a parishioner recalled the time she was at the dinner table with her family. There were four or five kids. Trying to be smart, she asked her dad, *"If the house were on fire, who would you save first, us kids or mom?"* Without a moment's hesitation he said, *"Why your mother of course!"* That is not the answer she was expecting, but from that time on she felt totally secure growing up.

The sacramental couple's vocation is to create an atmosphere of love between and around them that will touch the people in their lives. And we should want our couples to know it. It is their right. And we should want them to be humbled by it. But most of all, we want our couples to live it. Why? Because we need to see love like theirs at work in our church. Young people need to learn that love is something real. For if we can't turn to our sacramental couples to keep love alive, to whom shall we turn?

Dick and Barbara took a young woman into their home. She had bounced around from one foster home to another over the years, and along the way she got pregnant. Her stay would be till the baby was born, in only a few months, so the family did its best to help her. One daughter gave up her room so she could have some privacy. Being a dentist, Dick saw to her dental and medical needs. I'm sure Barbara took her shopping now and again, and probably to Disneyland with the other children.

After the baby was born, the family gathered for goodbyes. The young woman thanked everyone for the love and respect she had received from them and for their support, especially to the daughter who had given up her room, as well as for the good times. Then she turned directly to Dick and Barbara and said, *"I want to thank you for everything, but especially for the way you love each other. Before coming here, I thought love was just a word people used so they could take advantage of others, like me. But the way you obviously love each other, you have made love something I can believe in. Thanks!"*

Dick and Barbara made love real for this young woman. I happened to visit the family several years later, and by coincidence, the young woman was also there visiting. The Sacrament of Matrimony had changed her life. Such is the power of sacramental love at work.

Our couples don't have to talk about it or even consciously try to witness to it. They just need to live it. Jesus present in their love will do the rest. Sadly, those who marry outside the church have absolutely no idea of the crucial place they could play in God's plan to form and shape our world. This has to change!

* * * * * * *

Oh yes, that reminds me. Why does the Catholic Church require Catholics to follow church law if they want their marriage to be recognized by the church? It is because it assumes that Catholics have a special relationship to the Catholic Church that began when they were baptized into Christ. Once they were baptized they became a part of the world of grace, reborn as it were, into the family of God. They became part of the new creation, for when they came up out of the baptismal waters they were dead to sin and alive to God in Christ Jesus.(Rom. 6:11) This is all predicated on the truth of faith that baptism means something and the church takes it seriously!

But the newly baptized not only have a relationship with Jesus through their baptism, they also have a relationship with all others members of the family of God, their brothers and sisters in Christ. Even though many Christian churches seem to imply that Christianity is only a "me and Jesus" affair, we as Catholics don't. It is "me and Jesus and us" affair, not a private, individual relationship one just has with Jesus. From the time of their baptism on, they are expected to learn what it means to be a part of the Catholic family and to live lives in keeping with their calling as members of God's household. This is especially true when they marry, as they will have a special place, a unique role in the life of that family, a sacramental presence necessary for the growth and life of the church. And the church takes this very seriously, too.

When Catholics marry outside the church, they consciously or unconsciously totally ignore this new creation, this graced reality, and their special relationship with the people of the church. It's like some people, who, when getting married, disregard their families by not even inviting them to the wedding. In reality, when Catholics who truly understand their faith marry outside the church, they are saying, in effect, *"You as my brothers and sisters in Christ don't matter to me. Forget about our spending our love for you."* So, when the church does not recognize their marriage, it is because, either wittingly or unwittingly, they didn't recognize the church and their relationship with the church when they went through the marriage ceremony. They committed to a way of life that excluded the church entirely, like they wanted nothing to do with it. Even if they believe they entered a covenant with God and with each other, there is no covenant with God's People.

Not being allowed to receive Holy Communion, rather than a punishment, is a way the Church tries to underscore the importance of each Catholic's relationship with the People of God, and that ignoring it by marrying outside the church is not a matter of indifference. The fact that they have ignored their relationship with the other members of the church is not a minor thing. Because, by doing so, they estrange themselves from the community of faith and, by that act, choose to remove themselves from the Eucharistic table. After all, receiving Holy Communion is the highest expression of our unity not only with God but also with one another as members of the community of faith.

My observation is that very few who marry outside the church realize what they have done. But all is not lost. When reconciliation has taken place with the People of God, which normally comes with regularizing of the marriage in the Church and receiving the Sacrament of Reconciliation, the person is then, once again, welcomed to the Eucharistic table. But it should be noted that getting one's marriage "blessed" in the church is not the "ticket" to Holy Communion. It is their "ticket" to once again be back in a healthy relationship with the assembly, the People of God. That is what gives them and everyone else access to the table.

"The kingdom of heaven is like a merchant's search for fine pearls. When he found one really valuable pearl, he went back and put up for sale all he had to buy it" (Matt: 13:45). The Sacrament of Matrimony is such a pearl; and yet we step right over it and keep going, looking for something else that will give meaning, purpose and joy to our marriages. Couples seek out exotic places to celebrate their weddings to make them special. But if they could see the gift they are receiving and the gift they are becoming in the Sacrament of Matrimony, such efforts would be seen as missing the point as to what it is really all about. Marrying in the church is about bringing the kingdom of God to earth as it is in heaven. Yes, we take the Sacrament of Matrimony seriously as part of the sacred treasury of the church! If that should also come as a surprise, or if you still wonder what difference it makes, I urge you to read on.

CONVERSATION STARTERS:

1. Why did you get married in the Catholic Church?

2. What did you want for yourself when you married?

3. What did you want for your spouse?

4. What did you want for the Church?

5. Where do you find support for your vocation as a sacramental couple?

CHAPTER TWO

A MATRIMONAL SPIRITUALITY

"What did "He" want?"

Sven and his wife Lena were having, let's say, "intimacy problems." Actually, Sven was, so he went to a sex therapist for some advice. After a thorough examination the therapist said to Sven, *"All I think you need is some exercise and you should be fine. I recommend that you walk a couple of miles a day for a month and then call me to let me know how things are going."* So Sven walked two miles a day, and at the end of 30 days called the therapist as he had been told. *"And how is your sex life now?"* asked the therapist. *"How vud I know,"* said Sven, *"I'm 60 miles from home."*

* * * * * * *

Sometimes, doing what we are told may miss the point altogether, as is the case with poor Sven. It is imperative that we are clear in the guidance we give people and in what we ask them to do. For example, I would certainly hate to think the church is hesitant to encourage young people to enter the Sacrament of Matrimony, but, as we've indicated, there doesn't seem to be a whole lot of enthusiasm around it. Granted, it may be good to advise them not to marry when too young, but not to talk about the vocation of matrimony really doesn't help. Who knows, some might think that talking about marriage might somehow push them to think too much about sex. Believe me, they're thinking about it already. A grandfatherly friend of mine was asked by a young man, *"What do you think about premarital sex?"* He answered, *"When I was your age, I thought about it all the time."* Sexual images saturate our culture, so we can't pretend they aren't having an impact. The task before us is to counter the prevailing attitudes about sex that can be so damaging to the human soul, not by ignoring them, but by appreciating the gift that sex is, especially in the committed relationship of marriage. Furthermore, encouraging young couples to consider sacramental marriage doesn't mean they need to be in any hurry to get married. But we do want them to know that when they do marry, being married in the Catholic Church is an important way for them to live out their Catholic faith and their commitment to Christ.

I have a friend who went through a time when she wished she was a nun. Her inner urgings came a little late as she had a husband and six children. She would go to the convent for Mass during the week and sit with the nuns in church on Sundays. While she had a genuine desire to grow in holiness, she was going about it in totally the wrong way. As a married woman, she was called to matrimonial spirituality, not monastic spirituality. Apparently, she had come to believe that true holiness was not possible for married people. If so, I'm afraid it was not totally her fault.

I think it is shame that we don't have very many married people canonized as saints. We have most often identified holiness with hermits, priests, apostles, founders of religious orders, missionaries, Carmelite nuns and the like. And they have been held up to us as models of holiness for us to emulate. Most of them were celibate or they took the vow of consecrated virginity. Furthermore, many of the canonized saints, who had been married somewhere along the way, were not noted so much for what they did during their marriages but for what they did after their spouse had died, like St. Elizabeth Ann Seton, who converted to Catholicism and then founded Catholic Schools in the United States. Still other married saints vowed to live together as celibates. I'm not saying the church is wrong in canonizing them nor am I saying they are not saints worthy of emulation. What I am saying is that while we can learn much from them, they are not relatable models to the kind of holiness that married people, as married people, are called to. Some might even get the mistaken impression that sex and holiness are not compatible; that a "sexual saint" is an oxymoron. For this reason, may I refer you to the words of St. Francis de Sales in his classic book on spirituality The Introduction to the Devout Life.

> I say that devotion must be practiced in different ways by the nobleman and the working man, by the servant and the prince, by the widow, by the unmarried girl and by the married woman. But even this distinction is not sufficient; for the practice of devotion must be adapted to the strength, to the occupation and to the duties of each in particular. Tell me... whether it is proper for a bishop to want to lead a solitary life like a Carthusian; for married people to be more concerned than a Capuchin about increasing their income; for a working man to spend his whole day in church like a religious; or on the other hand for a religious to be constantly exposed like a bishop to all the events and circumstances that bear on the needs of our neighbor. Is not this sort of devotion ridiculous, unorganized and intolerable? Yet, this absurd error occurs very frequently, but in no way does true devotion... destroy anything at all. On the contrary, it perfects and fulfills all things. In fact, if it ever works against, or is inimical to, anyone's legitimate station and calling, then it is very definitely false devotion... True devotion does still better. Not only does it not injure any sort of calling or occupation, it even embellishes and enhances it.[1]

If married people are expected to become saints, it will be as married men and married women, as husbands and wives, fathers and mothers, not something or someone else! The vows they make on their wedding day to be true to each other *"in good times and bad, in sickness and health; to love and honor each other all the days for their lives,"* are no less sacred than a Trappist monk's or a Carmelite nun's vows to live poverty, chastity and obedience all the days of their lives. And crucial to a married couple's holiness is their sexual relationship. Being consecrated to love one's spouse in marriage is in no way a lesser consecration than that to virginity. In some ways it may even be more difficult to live out. Some have even said that a couple's sexual intimacy is the human foundation to the sacramentality of their marriage. Be that as it may, it is too bad if our married couples haven't heard this before. You see, rediscovering the sacredness of sacramental marriage involves discovering the sacredness of their sexual relationship. To some, this may come as a complete surprise.

* * * * * * *

Many people are intimidated by the concept of spirituality. Maybe an insight by the Jesuit anthropologist Teilhard de Chardin will help. He said, *"We are not human beings struggling to be spiritual, but spiritual beings struggling to be human."* We were created in the image of that God who existed for all eternity, that spiritual being who was enfleshed in Jesus. This means that we are all spiritual beings created and enfleshed at the moment of conception. Our task in life is to become human, just like Jesus did in the incarnation when he was conceived. We say we want to be more spiritual, and that is good. But the irony is this. The evidence that we have become more spiritual is not that we bow deeper before receiving Holy Communion or make bigger signs of the cross when we pray, but that we have become more human. We become more compassionate, loving, forgiving, faithful, courageous and caring. That is to say, we become more like Jesus. The only way we can live out being spiritual is through our humanity. We become more human, "better" human beings.

To become more human, the only thing Jesus had to overcome was his immaturity, so *"he grew in wisdom, age and grace before God and man"* (Luke 2:52). For most of us, the biggest thing holding us back is sin; the original sin we were born with and the sins we have committed all by ourselves. You see, sin distorts our humanity. It warps it into something less than what we were created to be. Think of fun house mirrors, except that the distortions to our humanity from sin are nothing to laugh at. In fact, some sins are so violent and horrible that we even say, *"Whoever did that is inhuman."* Jesus shows us what the "spiritual made human" is meant to look like. That's why Jesus says, *"Follow me,"* and *"Learn from me for I am meek and humble of heart."* How human we become depends on how we respond to Jesus' invitations.

Becoming more spiritual seems more within reach of the ordinary person when we think of it as becoming more human. When growing up I wondered what would happen if I became more spiritual and saintly. Would I start to levitate, get the stigmata or something extraordinary like that? Boy, that's out of reach for me. But if becoming more holy means becoming more loving, forgiving and understanding it isn't. With God's help, I can do that. So can you. The Holy Spirit empowers us to become better human beings, to live more in the spirit of Jesus.

In marriage, being more human is especially called for at those times when couples are most vulnerable with each other, and when most is at stake for their life together and for their family. And I can think of no time more important than when our couples are sexually intimate with each other. Sexual intimacy is meant to be a human act above all else, not just an animal act. It calls for love, tenderness, care, sensitivity and respect, while being at the same time generative and responsible; which flow from a couple's commitment to each other and to their future together. It requires couples who are willing to accept the natural consequences of their intimacy. Rather than being about using one's spouse in a selfish way, it is more akin to a genuine surrendering of oneself to the other in love. When viewed this way, sexual activity outside of a committed, marital relationship will in some way be less than "fully human." But by the same token, it can be truly a holy and sacred act for our married couples, a time when the spiritual and physical, divine and human are in harmony as one. It was St. Irenaeus in the second century who said, *"The glory of God is the human person fully alive."* There is no reason why this is not true for our couples when experiencing sexual intimacy.

* * * * * * *

I don't mind hearing a woman say, *"My husband is my best friend."*
But without their committed sexual relationship, they would just be best
friends. Our married couples are more than friends. They are living
sacraments of the Church. It is good to remember that the spiritual is not
so much the opposite of the physical as it is that force which transforms
the physical and enables it to point to deeper more beautiful realities. For
example, Jesus took ordinary bread and transformed it by his love for us
into a sign that points to a hunger in us only he can satisfy. Similarly,
when surrounded by responsible, selfless love, the sexual desire between a
husband and wife enables them to experience an absorption in each other
that has often been described as ecstasy. Interestingly, that is the same
word that describes the spiritual experience of mystics when absorbed in
the love of God. Spiritual writers will even say that such love can take a
couple to the "threshold of heaven." Granted, if you are married, you are
probably saying to yourself, *"Whoever said that must be a celibate."*
Maybe so, but my point here is to help you get over any lingering thought
that sex is dirty, unbecoming of holy people, or that, because you're
married, you are somehow less than those called to the priesthood or
religious life. Good grief, when I was in the seminary we jokingly called
the track of theology that dealt with sex *"de dirtibus."*

Sexual desire is at the very heart of a couple's spirituality as a couple.
It cannot be separated from their way of life. It is at the core of their way
of life. Clearly, we are not limiting sexuality to genital activity here. On
the contrary, it is an attitude of mind and heart that permeates every aspect
of a couple's relationship. It affects their openness to each other
throughout the day; their readiness to listen when the other needs to be
heard; their willingness to share hopes, fears, dreams and disappointments,
and to empathize with their spouse's feelings. When the sexual desire
between a husband and wife is strong, there is no room for selfishness,
manipulation, egoism or the quest for personal satisfaction or self-
fulfillment at the other's expense. Or, as Father Chuck Gallagher, S.J.,
who was instrumental in the rapid growth of Worldwide Marriage

Encounter, often put it, *"The quality of a couple's sexual relationship is a barometer of their overall relationship."*

A young woman whose husband was not facing into his drinking problem came to see me. She said that they argue, fight and brood. I asked her the last time they had been sexually intimate. She thought for a moment and said, *"About a year ago."* Their marriage was in trouble. The problem was alcohol. The symptom was sexual distance.

On the other hand, there is the story of the couple who came up to their pastor and asked, *"Is it okay to have sex before receiving Holy Communion?"* The priest looked at them for a moment and said, *"I suppose, as long as you don't block the aisle!"* Now don't get upset. It's just a story, but it does make the point. I would imagine that couples who share Eucharist after having been intimate together experience a greater sense of unity in Christ after receiving Eucharist. Why wouldn't they?

And for those who think such images are inappropriate for church, I recommend they attend the Holy Saturday Easter Vigil and then listen and watch closely during the blessing of the baptismal water. The priest prays:

> **May this water receive by the Holy Spirit**
> **the grace of your Only Begotten Son,**
> **so that human nature . . . may be found worthy**
> **to rise to the life of newborn children**
> **through water and the Holy Spirit.**

Then he lowers the large Easter Candle three times into the water, as he continues:

> **May the power of the Holy Spirit . . .**
> **Come down through your Son into**
> **the fullness of this font . . .**

Clearly, this action is meant to have phallic overtones as the new baptismal water is symbolically "impregnated" by the power of the Holy

Spirit. The baptismal font is even referred to as the "womb of the church," as it is from there that the new children of God are born into the life of grace. The church brings the images of the sexual and the sacred together through these liturgical actions since, by their nature, there is no reason why they shouldn't be.

Think about this for a moment. In the Trinity, it is the Son who reveals the Father to us. We know Jesus by his interaction with the Father. It is their mutual love that reveals the Holy Spirit. Each person of the Trinity is revealed and understood only in relationship to the other persons. We cannot really know one person without knowing the other persons also. The nature of the Trinitarian relationship does not allow otherwise. The same is true of the nature of a sacramental couple's relationship. It is their loving interaction with each other and sexual desire for each other that not only maintains their unity of intimacy, it develops and deepens it. This is neither suspended from nor dispensed with when they are apart, like when one is away on a business trip. When a husband is filled with his spouse, why would he ever hide the fact that he is married?

"Lovemaking" is a good word. It is so much more than a means to pleasure and the reduction of tensions, although these are certainly not bad. Through sexual intimacy, a couple, literally, make more love. Sometimes that love is enfleshed in children, but it should always generate deeper intensity of love in the couple. This reminds me of the time Oly said to Sven who had five sons, *"You got a boy every time."* *"Oh no,"* said Sven. *"Sometimes ve didn't get anything."*

However, when lovemaking does not express the way of life for the couple, that is, when they are not making love in the many other ways open to them throughout the day, such as by their tenderness, sensitivity, attention, mutual respect or when their sexual intimacy is seen only as a regrettable duty, it is less likely to "make love." In fact, it probably won't. The issue in this case is not the appropriateness of the couple's sexual intimacy as much as the likely inappropriateness of their way of life together and the inadequate expression of their desire for each other throughout the day. That behavior is what may not be befitting their dignity as a married couple. A friend of mine tells of the time when, after a fight with his wife, he said to himself, *"17 years of marriage and she still does know how much I love her."* He knew he needed to find even more ways to let her know.

If sexual intercourse is not integrated into the total life of the couple, it becomes an isolated event, disconnected from its source of power to give life. Guys will want it just for their own pleasure and satisfaction, not for the purpose of showing their wives how much they love them. That is about as life-giving as macho boasts of "scoring." Nor is sexual intercourse meant to be used as a means to an end, such as withholding it as a punishment or doling it out as a reward. Truly, this is sexual exploitation; perhaps the most common, though seldom mentioned, form of sexual abuse. I recall hearing the confession of a man whose wife had stopped having sex with him three years earlier. His hurt was so great he couldn't help crying as he mentioned it. He was a victim of sexual abuse! A couple's sexual relationship is so important that both parties must take responsibility for it. If it is the wife's call all the time, then the guy will ask all the time. It's like the guy who woke up his wife at two o'clock in the morning and handed her a glass of water and an aspirin. *"What's this for?"* she asked. *"I don't have a headache."* To which her husband replied, *"I was hoping you'd say that!"*

But it has to be so much more than physical intimacy. After all, it is only an expression of what is going on between the couple. Sadly, there is a lot of sex without human intimacy at all. The unity that God wants to have with all humanity is a unity of love. For example, people can be united *against* a common enemy, even united *in hate* of an enemy. That is not the unity that God wants for us. It must be born of love. That is the kind of unity expressed by a loving couple when they are physically intimate with each other. Above all, God reveals himself to us through love. It is trans-rational, beyond reason. Unity comes when there is no longer space between a husband and wife, only the oneness of shared love. By contrast, this reveals how the tragedy of rape violates a person physically, psychologically and spiritually. It cannot express love. It is an empty, violent lie! By the same token, so-called "recreational sex" may have nothing to do with love either, and thus dehumanizes and cheapens this most wonderful and meaningful of human acts. I wonder, when we experience true love in any of its forms, do we get a "glimpse" of God, a "taste" of the divine? I would think so, and it can keep us going. There is no doubt in my mind that God is present in the intimate expression of love between a husband and wife. And because God is present there, it can be seen as that dimension of their life that generates the power of love that gives them life as a couple.

* * * * * * *

Again, for a husband and wife just to be best friends is not enough. When sexual intimacy is intentionally excluded from the relationship, it says, *"For now I'll be your friend, not your spouse."* This is a form of infidelity, an adulteration of the marital covenant and an affront to their spirituality as a sacrament of the church. You see, infidelity is not just a matter of improper involvement with someone not your spouse. It is also a matter of improper non-involvement with one's own spouse. Infidelity isn't just what happens in someone else's bed. It's also what's not happening in your own. Think about it. Infidelity is a cruel way of saying to one's spouse, *"I don't believe in you anymore."* That is why it is so devastating. Another surprise?

But what of the couple who choose to live as brother and sister, especially if recommended to do so by a spiritual director? If they have any intimacy between them, it's hard to imagine what it would be, and intimacy of some form is necessary for a healthy human being. Both would have to be extraordinary people and totally committed Christians who both unwaveringly agree to this arrangement. It's hard for me to imagine what the reasons might be that call for such a celibate relationship without flirting in some way with the notion that sex is somehow unholy. To recommend such a practice for a couple is a rather sobering thought. It is hard for me to see how it could help them grow spiritually as a couple.

To put all of this in a slightly different way, how would parents like it if I baptized their baby with smelly, muddy water? Among other things, it would be a crummy sign of cleansing from sin. Well, what kind of sign of Christ's love are our couples when they grow distant from each other?

We need to thank our couples for struggling to love each other when it's hard to do so. Forgive me if I'm too idealistic about the Sacrament of Matrimony and the sacredness of those called to this wonderful vocation. Yet, lay people are just as idealistic about priests and how we should live. Turnabout is fair play.

> A woman came to see me to say that she loved her husband and he loved her, but there wasn't much joy in their marriage. She said it was like a 7-Up gone flat. *"What should I do?"* she asked. In a moment of inspiration, I told her, *"Do what you did the first year you were married."* *"Like what?"* she asked further. *"I don't know,"* I said, *"I wasn't there."*

> A week later, she came up to me at our coffee hour after Mass and said excitedly, *"It worked!"* *"What worked?"* I asked trying to recall our earlier visit. *"I did what you suggested. I treated my husband the way I did the first year we were married. I spent time with him after he got home from work. I fixed myself up a bit and put on a little "foo foo" juice. Stuff like that. And when he left for work one morning I gave him a kiss. He gave me a peck on the cheek back. I asked him, 'What if this is the last kiss we'll ever have?' He gave me a really big one and left for the car with a big smile on his face. I think he was eager to get home that night."*

Life and love were back in their relationship. I wonder how the woman would have answered me if I had asked her if she felt closer to God before she came to see me the first time in my office or later at the coffee hour. I would like to believe she would have said, *"At the coffee hour."* After all, where love is, God is. While we may not always feel it or even recognize it as holiness, when it's there we are touching the divine.

CONVERSATION STARTERS:

1. Is the concept of a matrimonial spirituality new to you? How?

2. What makes intimacy life-giving for you?

3. What difference do children make?

4. Does your spouse know how much you love her/him?

5. Do you have a patron saint that is particularly helpful to you as a married person?

---

1. The Introduction to the Devout Life, St. Francis de Sales. Part 1, chapter 3

CHAPTER THREE

ENTERING THE MYSTERY

"We're invited to a dance."

An older couple was spending a quiet evening at home. The husband was concerned about his wife's apparent hearing loss and decided to test it without her realizing what he was doing. As she is standing at the kitchen sink he sneaks up behind her and from about ten feet away asks, *"Do you love me?"* But she doesn't say anything. So he gets a little closer and asks again, *"Do you love me?"* Still there was no response. So finally he leans right into her ear and says, *"Do you love me?"* She turns to him and says, *"For heaven's sake, Henry, for the third time, yes!"*

* * * * * *

While it is good not to take important things for granted, it is also important that we have ears to hear. Rediscovering the significance of the Sacrament of Matrimony also requires an awakening of our faith. For example, in the last chapter we made reference to the Holy Trinity. If that is all we did, just give a respectful nod toward the Trinity in passing, it would be a grave oversight. In fact, it would ignore the very foundation of what I want to say in this book. Just saying that we believe in the Trinity isn't enough, but it seems that that is all we have been doing for years. It was the respected theologian Karl Rahner, S.J. who observed the following: *"Should the doctrine of the Trinity have to be dropped as false tomorrow, the major part of religious literature would remain virtually unchanged."* To this, Father Richard Rohr observes, *"And 95% of our lives would remain unchanged."*[1]

It seems that the Trinity, which is at the very heart of our Christian concept of God, has been either ignored over the years as irrelevant or it has been misunderstood altogether, apparently, with neither pastoral nor practical value for the Christian life. We wonder how this can be possible since the doctrine of the Trinity is *the* central dogma of our Catholic Faith. The Trinity is not just one doctrine amid many doctrines, equal in importance, let's say, to the incarnation, to the Eucharist and to the church. On the contrary, it is that doctrine out of which all other doctrines arise. Notice how the Nicene Creed we profess at Mass is constructed. First, we say we believe in God the Father and then in the Father's work as creator. Then we say we believe in Jesus Christ, and then in his works as redeemer. And finally, we say we believe in the Holy Spirit and then in the works of the Spirit as sanctifier. Without the Trinity the Nicene Creed, as we know it, would never have been written.

Unfortunately, we also hear people say things like, *"The Trinity is a mystery we can't explain, so we just have to believe it."* By saying that, it's as if they want to set the doctrine of the Trinity on the coffee table with other lovely but irrelevant things to gather dust. From Rahner's observation, it appears that too many Christian writers have done just that. My discovery of the significance of the Sacrament of Matrimony flows from my discovery of the significance of the doctrine of the Trinity.

Yes, the Trinity is a mystery, but that doesn't mean it can be relegated to an afterthought, a disposable footnote to our understanding of Christianity. It is a mistake to just say that a mystery is something we cannot understand, as if that dispenses the human mind from trying to comprehend what that something is. I like to think that a mystery is something so big, so vast, that we simply cannot get our finite minds around it. It's too "immense," if you will. For example, I cannot get my mind around the concepts of limitless space or endless time, either. For me those concepts are mysteries. But that doesn't mean we can't know something about space and time. Granted, we are forced to speak of the Trinity in metaphors and similies, but that gives us insight enough to offer us a limited understanding of what the Trinity is like. Granted, every human attempt to comprehend the Trinity in its fullness will fall short, but what we have come to learn from our efforts to unravel this mystery is truly extraordinary.

We are fortunate to live at a time of renewed interest and scholarship around the doctrine of the Trinity. I was introduced by Father Richard Rohr, O.F.M. to the late Catherine LaCugna's wonderful book ***God For Us***.[2] If the Trinity is as important as he made it sound, I needed to read her book. When I did, I said to myself, *"What a shame I didn't hear this stuff years ago. Why has it taken so long?"* Needless to say, it resulted in a paradigm shift, not only in my view of the Trinity, but also in my understanding of the Christian life. Much of what I will be saying here is drawn largely, though not exclusively, from both LaCugna's book and from Rohr's reflections on it. If I make any worthwhile contribution, it will be in my efforts to connect this all to our understanding of the Sacrament of Matrimony. And what we can know of the Trinity serves as the key to unlocking the magnificence of this pearl of great price.

* * * * * *

What follows is not New Age theology, although it may sound like that to some. On the contrary, it goes back to the earliest days of the church. The early church fathers had an interesting Greek word to describe the dynamic, inner life of the Trinity, *perichoresis*. In the seminary I learned the Latin word, *circumincession*. For me, these high powered words needed to be unpacked so I could understand them. According to Father Rohr, the Cappadocian Fathers in the early church came to think of that inner, dynamic life of the Trinity as a dance. That is to say, the inner life of God, the flow of life going on among the Father, Son and Holy

Spirit now and for all eternity is like a dance. God is not a dancer. God is the dance. Such is the nature of that divine being we call God. When God created us as human beings, in the divine image, we were given the unique capacity to enter into the life of the Trinity, that is, to enter into the eternal dance.

Now this is something I could get my mind around, although dancing has always been a bit of a mystery to me as well. Nonetheless, it is a good image and speaks some wonderful truths. A good dancer is not only one who knows all the steps. Somehow the "spirit" of the dance must get into the dancer. That became evident to me by just watching a few episodes of the television show *"Dancing with the Stars."* Those who "got it," expressed the spirit of the dance, not just the steps. The flow of the dance took over their bodies as though the dancers actually surrendered themselves into the flow, the rhythm of the dance. And in that act of surrender, they became better dancers.

A dance is also something that goes on between dancers. It is an expression of the relationship that exists between the dancers. It's hard to think of Fred Astaire without seeing Ginger Rogers or Cyd Charisse dancing with him. In fact, it is the dynamic of their relationship while dancing together that makes it so beautiful. If they are not constantly aware of each other throughout the dance, it would fall apart. One dancer is always seen in relationship to the other. Something is happening between them. So, too, the power of God exists in the relationship that exists between the persons of the Trinity. The persons are never in isolation from each other. If they were, the divine dance would fall apart, too.

Father Michael Himes from Boston College, another respected theologian, gives us further insight into this mystery of God. He says that the least imperfect way of describing the life of the Trinity, since all ways are inadequate, is the insight from St. John's first epistle: *"God is love"* (1 John 4:8). Again, God is not a being that loves. God is the love! For all eternity divine love exists; divine love is happening. And when God chooses to express that love outside of God, as it were, we have what we call grace. Grace is the action of God's love outside of God that creates, redeems, forgives, comforts, unites and gives life. The reason St. Paul could claim, *"Love does not come to an end."* (1 Cor. 13:7) is because it never had a beginning. Love has existed for all eternity; it is the very core of "being." Might not this also be the reason St. John said, *"Where love is God is?"*

While the mystery remains, it is clear that we are invited into this mystery. But as we enter into the way of love, Love also enters into us. It becomes a part of us. As St. John says, *"We abide in God and God in us"* (1 John 4:13). While great theologians have found ways to reveal and open this up for us, Blessed Elizabeth of the Trinity discovered it on her own through prayer. As she says, *"I surrender myself to You as Your prey. Bury Yourself in me so I may bury myself in You."* [3] This may not be the way we would say it, but the idea is the same.

When we deal with mystery, we need not just think of things that are extraordinary. There is endless mystery in the ordinary all around us, for example, the mystery of life. To me it is so much greater than the mystery of death. Life is the mystery that surrounds us every day. How did we get here? What does it mean? How did it happen that we have fresh air to breathe and beautiful sunsets to watch? How is it that we can stand in awe looking into the vast universe of the night sky, or a swallow swooping to the lake's surface to catch a flying gnat? How is it that we became a part of it, with the ability to marvel at it? When we stop to look at it, we see that even the ordinary is extraordinary after all. And then mix in the wonder of love, something that cannot be measured by any instrument of science, and we begin to sense that we may be getting close to the divine source of it all. Where love is, God is! That is the mystery.

St. Bonaventure said that *"the Trinity leaves its imprint or stamp on everything, on all creation."* [4] Father Richard Rohr speaks of the "family resemblance" that exists between the creator and all of creation, in which all express the wonder of God in some way. But our human family resemblance is unique, as we are made in the image of God. Now, the resemblance we humans have is not based on our physical features, but in the kind of relationship we have with one another. The original intent of God was that it be a relationship of love. But sin got in the way. To make a very long story short, Jesus came to restore what was lost, as evidenced in his words, *"By this all will know you are my disciples, your love for one another"* (John 13:35).

What holds everything together is how they are related. Nothing exists in isolation. Everything is in a relationship with something else, from the smallest atom to the galaxies of the universe. In an atom, protons, neutrons and electrons act in relationship to each other, and the power that exists between them boggles the human mind. (Think atomic bomb.) The moon in orbit around planet earth is held there by the gravity of the earth and the pull of the sun. Should our earth suddenly lose its gravitational pull, the moon would soon experience a fiery death. Why is it that way and not some other way? While science can address how things work, it cannot answer the question why they exist at all. And again, add that dimension of faith which introduces the notion of a loving creator and says that we human beings are made in the image of God, and it is as though we step through a looking glass into a whole new wonderland of mystery.

* * * * * *

Life either has meaning, or it is absurd. It has a purpose, or it is pointless. When standing before the wonder of it all, the greatest minds are reduced to ask the question of a child: why? Science can't seem to answer it. This is not the fault of science, just evidence of its limitations. Yet, there is something about the human creature that can't help but wonder what the purpose in life is. It's a question that arises from deep inside of us as human beings today as it has arisen in the hearts of men and women for thousands of years. It has to be something that will resonate with people everywhere, regardless of culture, race or even religion. And for that purpose to make any sense at all, it must be something that will hold life together in times of joy and sadness, victory and defeat, uncertainty and peace.

For me, that purpose would have to be like a key that opens the door to the joy and meaning in life. It would give us a sense of well being and purpose regardless of what is going on around us, a peace that no one can take from us. It would be that center out of which we will live our lives each day, whether we do big things or small, important or insignificant. And in all cases, if we live in keeping with our dignity as people created in the image of God, whatever we do would give life.

Great people over the centuries have tried to answer this "purpose of life" question, some more successfully than others. And of course, some not so great people have tried to answer it as well, again, some more successfully than others. For example, when young, our purpose in life was often just to get rich, to become famous or maybe powerful. But as we grow older, we realize that such achievements would neither last nor ultimately satisfy. In fact, most of us will resign ourselves to those 15 minutes of fame that Andy Warhol spoke of, being lucky if we get anything near that much time. Besides, the possession of wealth, fame and power do not offer us much consolation at our bedside when life is slipping through our fingers. We can't take them with us when we die. They simple do not satisfy the deepest longings of the human heart.

In Shakespeare's play **Richard III,** the desperate king pleads in despair on the battlefield, *"A horse, a horse; my kingdom for a horse."* How worthless and irrelevant all his power and possessions had become! That is why there is no one more to be pitied than the person who climbed the ladder of success only to find out that when he got to the top he had placed the ladder against the wrong wall. Acquiring such things as power, possessions and privilege can't be our purpose in life as human beings because only a small percentage of people would be able to achieve such a purpose, which is not within the reach of all. Most would die failures. But even more so, even those who "had it all" could not take any of it with them when they die. So we must find a purpose in life that is within reach of everyone, an answer that is worthy of our dignity as human beings created in the divine image, and one that we can take with us when we die.

I believe that the answer to the purpose in life has been handed to us. It is such a simple answer that it can easily be missed altogether, especially when we have found so many ways to ignore it, not to mention outright fight it. We seem not to want it. Yet, as simple as it is, we hear almost no one say it. But some have. St. Augustine put it like this; speaking to God,

"Our hearts are restless until they rest in Thee." St. John of the Cross put it more simply. *"In the evening of life we will be judged on love."* Blessed Mother Teresa of Calcutta said it even more simply still. *"Do little things with great love."* An answer that resonates with me can be stated in one simple sentence. *"We are on this earth to learn how to love."* If we fail to learn how to love, we fail "Humanity 101." And love is the one thing we can take with us when we die. The logic is simple.

> *We are made in the image of God who is love.*
> *The more we live in the spirit of love, the closer we will come to living as we were created to live.*
> *Therefore, our purpose in life is to learn how to love.*

It fits with Augustine's longing of the human heart since we believe that God is love. Our hearts are restless until they have entered fully into the eternal flow or dance of divine love. And for John of the Cross, if we're going to be judged on how we have loved in life, then we'd better learn how to love. And according to Mother Teresa the way to make anything worthwhile is to make it an expression of love. Of course it was St. Paul who said, *"Without love, you are a noisy gong and a clanging symbol" (I Cor. 13:1).* In other words, to the degree we fail to live a life of love, to that degree we compromise our human dignity and we are *"worth nothing" (1 Cor. 13:3).* But when what we do in life expresses love, it will give life.

Since we were created in the divine image, and God is love, then the more completely we live a life of love (enter the dance of love), the closer we will be to living up to our dignity as human beings. Besides, isn't this the New Commandment that Jesus gave us at the Last Supper? Before that time, he said we were to love God with our whole heart, soul, mind and strength; our neighbor as ourselves. But now he tweaks it into something far more refined. *"**Love one another as I have loved you.**"* So, as Christians, we are not called just to love, but to love as Jesus has loved us. And so, we must know who this Jesus is and watch carefully how he lived. If we do, we will ultimately learn that to give of ourselves so others can live is the key to the Christian life if not the key to life itself. Then we will be living life in keeping with our dignity as creatures made in the divine image. Our "family resemblance" with the Trinity will be evident.

So, then, why are we on this earth? The old Baltimore Catechism asked it this way, *"Why did God make us?"* Remember the answer? *"God made us to know Him, love Him and serve Him in this life and to be happy with Him forever in the next."* While I still believe that, I also believe we could turn our answer around 180 degrees and look at it from God's perspective not ours, and it would still be correct. God made us so God could know *us*, love *us* and serve *us* in this life so God could be happy with *us* forever in the next. It all begins with God, especially our purpose in life. If God hadn't loved us first, we could never love God, or anything else for that matter.

* * * * * *

God sent his Son into the world to invite us back into the eternal flow of God's love lost at the time of the fall. Or to use that other metaphor for the inner life of God, Jesus came to invite us back into the eternal dance of God's love. Remember, as God is not one who loves but the love itself, God is not one who dances. God is the dance. We watch this Jesus throughout his life so we can learn the steps of the dance of love. Good dancers will not only hear the beat and rhythm of the music, but will allow that rhythm and music to somehow get inside of them, become a part of them. Similarly, to live in the flow of the dance of eternal love, the Spirit of this Jesus has to get inside of us. It needs to form and shape us little by little, week after week, year after year into people of the Divine Dance. And when our time is over, we will find ourselves dancing with the saints; with Mary, Joseph, Augustine, Theresa and with the entire heavenly host. It is possible for everyone, even the powerless and weak, perhaps especially the powerless and weak if we want to take the Beatitudes seriously *(Matt. 5:3-10)*. Truly, we will literally be dancing with the stars, but at a whole new level.

CONVERSATION STARTERS:

1. Why is the Trinity important to understanding sacramental marriage?

2. What brings the greatest joy to your relationship?

3. When you think of God, what image comes to mind?

4. Why is learning how to love the most important thing for us to learn?

5. Is the metaphor of the Trinity as a dance helpful for you as a couple? Why?

---

1. What Difference Does the Trinity Make," CD, Richard Rohr, O.F.M. (Mustard Seed Resource Center, Albuquerque, NM, 2004)

2. See, Catherine Mowry LaCugna, *God For Us*, The Trinity and the Christian Life (San Francisco: Harper Collins 1993)

3. Internet: Blessed Elizabeth of the Trinity (21 November 1904)

4. See, Anna Hunt, Trinity, Orbis Books 2005. p.106

CHAPTER FOUR

LOVE ME, LOVE ME NOT

"Honey, we need to talk."

Two brothers, eight and six years old, decided they were old enough to start swearing. They had heard others kids do it at school, so why shouldn't they? *"Do you know any swear words?"* the younger boy asked his brother. *"Well,"* he said, *"I heard a kid say 'hell' on the playground and other kids giggled. That must be one."* *"Yea, I bet it is. That's a good one." "Do you know any?"* the older brother asked. *"The teacher got after a kid for saying 'ass,' so that must be one, too." "Good, that should be enough for us to start,"* he said.

The next morning the two brothers were at the kitchen table and their mom asked, *"What would you boys like for breakfast?"* The older one said, *"Ah hell mom, I'll have some Cheerios."* With that, the mother grabbed the kid by the ear and marched him to the bathroom upstairs where she washed his mouth out with soap. The younger brother heard him bawling as she sent him to his room. When she came back down to the kitchen she asked, *"And what do you want?"* The little brother sat there with eyes open wide in a state of shock. *"Well,"* he answered, *"you can bet your ass it isn't Cheerios."*

* * * * * * *

I don't know what you think, but for me this is a story about innocence. Innocence comes from the Latin *"innocens,"* meaning without (*in*) harm (*nocens)*. Quite literally, the boys hadn't been wounded yet. They had no idea what the swear words meant, they just wanted to be like the older kids. While this story may be a bit crude for some peoples' sensitivities, we're going to talk about some things in this chapter that happen in homes everyday that are far worse, things so common that we may not even notice them anymore. Yet, they destroy innocence in far worse ways than by the use of crude language (which I certainly don't encourage). They inflict wound upon wound. What we say in this chapter will touch sensitivities also, but it needs to be said. To free the Sacrament of Matrimony to achieve its purpose in the church we must wake up to how we may be compromising it everyday.

As mentioned above, we are on this earth to learn how to love. In fact, we are programmed for love, to be sure, but our program has countless glitches in it. We are not perfect at love. Jesus was and Mary was, and maybe a few others, but that's about it. We are wounded people, sinners, limited in our love for others. Furthermore, much of what we call love is often just a charade, a distortion of the real thing. But before we can learn the ways of love, we have to learn what love is. For most of us, it will take time, maybe a lifetime. The process begins when we are small, infants even.

We have all heard those tragic stories of orphans from places like Rumania who were confined to nurseries with little or no interaction with others, no one to hold them, coo them or love them. As a result, they never developed as they should have, remaining psychologically and emotionally crippled, if not paralyzed for life. Because they never experienced love themselves, they never learned what love is, and therefore the ways of love. As a result, they had been wounded beyond repair even though they hadn't done anything wrong. I think we could agree that they were victims of a lack of love.

And this is a crucial point. Love is one of those things that can only be learned from the inside, as it were. It has to be experienced. By way of analogy, how do you describe the color red to a person born blind, or the colors of a rainbow? You can't. They must be experienced. We learn love from experiencing its coming to us from someone else. In time, we learn how to return it, but not immediately. Granted, we can learn *about* love from books, particularly from the gospel stories of Jesus, but knowing bible stories doesn't mean we have learned what love is or how to love. Who understands the ways of married love before they marry? No one I've ever met. (Couples who just live together don't know what married love is either. They can't.) As a celibate priest, I'll never know the experience of marital love. I have no idea what a new father feels when he holds his newborn. I know it's something special, maybe even beyond words to express, but I'll never know what it is because I haven't gone through the experience. I recall a young mother who said to her own mother one day, *"You never told me."* Somewhat puzzled by the comment, her mother asked in return, *"I never told you what?" "You never told me how much I would love my baby."* Of course she couldn't. The daughter had to learn it from experience.

Love wears many faces. We always want it to be joyful, uplifting, exciting, happy and fun. We want it to bring us a sense of wellbeing and inner peace. But it doesn't always work that way because there are some things about love we don't want to learn. Unavoidably, there is a downside to the experience of love. It can hurt like nothing else. We feel real pain when a child gets sick, when a husband goes off to war, or when a spouse dies, and there is absolutely no defense against it. The truth is, at the very moment we choose to love we open ourselves to pain and suffering. I think it is even safe to say that the way of love always leads to the cross. Our greatest joys and sorrows will come from the people closest to us, the ones we love, our spouse, our kids or whomever. If we didn't love them, we wouldn't feel that terrible fear when something threatens them or the awful pain when some misfortune hits them. Yet, we are made for love. It goes to the heart of who we are as human beings. We are even commanded to love. So, to choose to love can be risky, but the alternative is even more risky. Listen to C. S. Lewis:

> To love at all is to be vulnerable. Love anything, and your heart will certainly be wrung and possibly broken. If you want to make sure of keeping it intact, you must give your heart to no one, not even to an animal. Wrap it carefully round with hobbies and little luxuries; avoid all entanglements; lock it up safe in the casket or coffin of your selfishness. But in that casket – safe, dark, motionless, airless – it will change. It will not be broken; it will become unbreakable, impenetrable, irredeemable. The only place outside Heaven where you can be perfectly safe from all the dangers of love is hell. [1]

To enter the world of love is to enter a mystery. Love has the power to sweep us off our feet, to change our lives totally; it has the power to fill us with joy and to motivate us to do extraordinary things. While it can do all of this, it also has the power to crush us under its weight. Yet, we have no real alternative but to choose to love if we want to live life to the full, to experience what it means to be human.

* * * * * * *

Interestingly, almost every time Jesus said to his disciples, *"Do not be afraid,"* he was inviting them to let go of what they knew or thought they knew, so they could enter into the mystery he was trying to reveal to them. When he said, *"Follow me,"* knowing it would lead to the cross, he knew there was no other way than the way of love that could satisfy their deepest longings. He knew that that meant a future with pain in it, but he urged them to follow him anyway. There was no other way. *"Unless you take up your cross and follow me, you cannot be my disciple."* To follow Jesus is to follow the way of love, and it will always lead to the cross. He trusted that the disciples would learn from experience, as there is no other way to learn that perfect love casts out fear. *(cf. 1 John 4:17-21)*

In ordinary circumstances, who is more vulnerable than a husband who loves his wife or a wife who loves her husband? Both stand to be hurt by the other. Maybe this is why so many couples choose not to marry, so they can avoid this kind of vulnerability. When things get tough, they can just up and leave. But true love calls for commitment to one's beloved. It demands fidelity, a fidelity that frees each to surrender in love to the other. And even though there is still vulnerability present, there is also a unity that would otherwise be impossible. This unity leaves no room for competition or domination. Consequently, there is no need to fear. Truly, to enter into love, to surrender oneself to love, is to enter a mystery, a mystery we need not fear.

Father Richard Rohr speaks of the act of "falling in love." It isn't a rational thing at all, and the "falling" part may not last very long. But for as long as it lasts, its "victims" temporarily lose control of themselves; they let go, trusting they will be okay. It affords them the opportunity to gain a new perspective on life, a new way of seeing reality through the eyes of love.[2] And the reason they don't fear is because where love is God is, even though they may not be aware of this wonderful truth at all. By entering into this new experience of the divine flow of love, their world seems to turn upside down. It changes everything.

God wants us to learn how to love so we can experience life in all its richness, and thus discover how precious the gift of life really is. Learning the ways of love is the key to unlocking the mystery of life itself. And it is also by our living it that we will make love real in the world. Love is a reality that all people everywhere long for and should be able to experience and believe in. As we said earlier, being rich, powerful and having great prestige are not possible for all, but love is. In fact, the extraordinary benefits that come from love are possible for the simplest, humblest, most common people on this planet. This means that if the wealthy and powerful do not have love, in the words of St. Paul, *"... they have nothing"* (I Cor. 13: 2). The wealth, power and greatness of love come from what it creates between people. When love is what is passing back and forth between us, it has the power to transform us bit by bit into people who will image what it means to be fully human and fully alive. This is because we will have entered into the flow of divine love that grounds and surrounds us.

Having said all that, we now come to the point of this chapter, as well as the heart of a couple's vocation. I am convinced that the best place to experience love and to learn the fundamental ways of love is in the home. More than any other place, the finest school to learn the ways of love is our home, not our parish or our schools or even a kindergarten. It is in the family home where love, above all else, is meant to be in the air. I do not deny that real love does exist in our parishes and our schools, our kindergartens and even in the market place for that matter, and we can experience it there. But it will not be as powerful as the love we are meant to experience in our homes, especially when growing up.

No matter what we may learn about love elsewhere, if we experience genuine love in our families, with those closest to us, it will either enhance or trump those other experiences every time. And it is the husband and wife living the Sacrament of Matrimony who are empowered to create that atmosphere of love more than anyone else. It is the grace of the Sacrament of Matrimony that enables a married couple to generate the spirit of love, the kind of love Jesus commanded, in their homes. This goes to the heart of their call from God! How they fulfill this mission will be the most critical measure of their success as a married couple. I would confidently send any engaged couple into their home to observe and discover what real love looks like.

We now begin to see a bit more clearly how a married couple's love is not just for themselves, but also for others, in this case, their families. And most couples genuinely want to create a home where love is its hallmark. Unfortunately, tragically even, all too often there are things going on between a husband and wife, as well as others members of the family that destroy that atmosphere because their actions are incompatible with love. A man can't slap his wife in the face and say, *"I love you"* at the same time. The action contradicts the words. That is why such destructive dynamics going on between family members make love impossible to learn. It cannot be experienced.

* * * * * * *

I'm not sure if learning how to love is a pass/fail class or not, but when the children move out of their homes, they will either have the basics of love pretty much in place or they won't. To a great extent, their future will depend on which it is. While remedial work is possible, it is not always available or wanted. Knowing the form our love needs to take is not always obvious. Sometimes it is not clear what love will look like, especially in tough situations. Personally, I am uncomfortable asking myself that popular problem-solving question, *"What Would Jesus Do?"* It may work for some, but not for me. I don't know what Jesus would do since I am not Jesus and his ways are not my ways. It's too easy to fool myself into thinking I would know. Then I might be tempted to think that if someone disagrees with me they are also disagreeing with Jesus, and that would be manipulative.

But I can and do ask, *"What does love look like in this situation?"* At least that will express my desire to do what God wants me to do. It will be an expression of love for the here and now, although it may not turn out to be the best way I could have shown love. Love, you see, can wear many faces. Yet, whatever I do with love will be pleasing God because that is my desire. God knows my limits! With that assurance, then I do my best to figure out what that love should look like. Reassuring to this approach are the words of St Augustine. *"Love and do what you will. If you keep silence, do it out of love. If you cry out, do it out of love. If you refrain from punishing, do it out of love... Let the root of love be within. From such a root nothing but good can come."* To the extent we manifest the flow of divine love in our daily lives our actions will reflect the love and justice from which they spring. [3]

However, rather than try to show what love should look like, it may be more helpful to start by showing what love does NOT look like in certain situations. This will help make it obvious when love isn't present in our actions. I am not going to go into the details of those situations themselves, but, rather, how we often react to negative things that happen to us in ways that violate our commitment to love and thus make love almost impossible to teach and/or learn.

To underscore how serious this all is, we need to remember that our sacramental couples are more than models of what Christ's love looks like. They are empowered to bring Christ's love to bear upon what is happening to them and to their children in their home. Therefore, the way our couples deal with hurts and failings in their family's relationships carries a special weight. It can profoundly influence the kind of human beings their children turn out to be. What they do will either improve the quality of life in the home or weaken it. It is also in their power to destroy it.

Call them what you will, but those hurtful reactions that wound others are sins by any other name. They are the sins that can tear a family apart one little act at a time, and we may not even realize it. We are not talking adultery and murder here. They are too obvious. These sins are more subtle and sneaky. Often, they are evident in the way we react to things we don't like, things like human weakness, disappointment, a bad decision, a nagging fault, or maybe a hurt. Rather than bring healing, what we do makes things worse.

Drawing on a small booklet I wrote several years ago, [4] I am going to suggest that there are five deterrents to the development of healthy relationships that are particularly devastating to the family. To the degree these are present in a marriage to that degree they will neutralize the effectiveness of the couple as sacraments of the church and compromise the home as a school of love.

I am not ignoring all other family structures today, since what I am saying can be applied to them as well. But let me remind you that when a couple receives the Sacrament of Matrimony they are not just another married couple. They became a Sacrament *of* the Church, *by* the Church and *for* the Church. They became a living sign of Jesus' abiding presence in the Church. No other family structure can make that statement. That is not a put down of single parent families or non-sacramental marriages. It is a statement of our couples' special calling. Their vocation as sacramental couples is to enflesh in their lives the new commandment, *"Love one another as I have loved you."*

* * * * * * *

So, the first reaction to our brokenness that simply makes things worse is **anger**. I don't mean a passing, emotional kind of anger that quickly comes and goes. Rather, it is the kind of anger a spouse goes to bed with at night and gets up with in the morning. It smolders away waiting for an opportunity to break into flame. Caused by an unhealed hurt, perhaps, anger becomes a part of a person's make up, affecting attitudes, impairing judgment and distorting one's perception of reality. Everything is tainted by it. Verbal communication is destroyed. Listening is impossible. Sexual intimacy is empty, if there is any. When angry, one party starts looking for the other person's flaws and weaknesses and then the opportunity to exploit them in retaliation. This takes the classic form we call "the silent treatment" or the more subtle though sarcastic form of extreme politeness. *"Anything you say, dear."* One husband told me how he and his wife, over their many years of marriage, have developed non-verbal reactions that communicate volumes: a glance, the movement of a hand, an almost imperceptible shrug of the shoulders, an ever so slight turning away. Like a carefully aimed peccadillo, each is intended to inflict pain when it hits its mark.

Mind you, the cause of this anger may be a very real and unjustifiable hurt. This we concede. But we reject abiding anger as an appropriate response in marital and family relationships. No one has a right to inflict their anger on others, not just because of the pain and hurt it causes, but because it is totally incompatible with Jesus' commandment to love. *"Love does not brood over injuries."*

It was the end of the day when Pete and his wife had a bitter argument. Filled with anger and frustration, knowing he couldn't sleep next to her, he took a blanket and pillow and went to the living room couch to spend the night. As he lay there, looking up at the dark ceiling, his mind raced with all that had just happened. Then a thought struck him that caught him by surprise. It was that he and his wife were a living sacrament of the church and that in the morning their seven children would see them cold and distant from each other. Pete knew they deserved better, so he took his blanket and pillow and returned to the bedroom to resolve the conflict. It took them three hours, but they did it. The next morning their children saw a mother and a father who loved each other, although they looked awfully tired.

What motivated Pete to act was that he remembered their vocation as a sacrament of the Church. Because he did, they learned an important lesson about love that night. Love is incompatible with lingering anger, and the grace of matrimony calls them to get over it. They found a better way. We cannot embrace one another when we are embracing a hurt. We have to make a choice. Lose face or lose heart. (If you're thinking of things your spouse could be doing to make things better, don't forget the beam in your own eye.)

* * * * * * *

The second response to a hurt or a fault that destroys family relationships is **criticism**. If anger kills, criticism paralyzes. Criticism is the most common way of destroying another person's sense of self-worth. Through criticism we poison those we claim to love. Unlike legitimate correction, which is something mutually agreed upon by the people involved, and which is aimed at some action that someone has or has not done, criticism, as we are using it here, is an unsolicited attack on another's person intended as a "put-down." One couple suggests that our self-image is like a fresh sheet of paper. Each critical comment aimed at us rips away a little piece of that paper. Often, by the end of the day, the person's self image is just a little scrap. Using this image, we can see that there is no such thing as "constructive criticism." We can't build people up by tearing them apart.

There is a big difference between saying to your daughter, *"Your room is a mess,"* and saying, *"Only a slob could live in a room like that!"* Criticism, like abiding anger, is incompatible with love. There is no way to put someone down that will allow them to feel good about themselves. Yet, criticism has been raised to an art form in many of our families and in our church. It is practically a way of life for some. Criticism is the cancer of the Body of Christ, and it is out of control. While it is meant to change the other person, it begets defensiveness and retaliation. Nor can we stand up to criticism either. One word of criticism wipes out ten words of praise. Divorce has innumerable causes, but common to most is criticism. I believe that the epidemic of divorce in our society would virtually be stopped in its tracks if we stopped criticizing one another.

By the way, parents have no more right to criticize their children than anybody else. Criticism is probably the most widespread form of child abuse in society today. I recall a professor at Regis University in Denver say that the first law used to protect children from abuse by their parents was one on the books for the protection against cruelty to animals. We were all shocked to hear it, and we should have been. We have come a long way, but we still have a long way to go.

But parents do have a greater responsibility to praise and exalt their children. Praise and affirmation should be bouncing off the walls of our homes. If it's not, I don't see how a family can be joyful. And it could be a good indicator that a spirit of love is present in the family. Brothers and sisters owe this to one another, too. I still have bruises on my arms to prove that I grew up with three older brothers, but the worst I can remember being called by a brother was a "sissy" for not grabbing a stinging nettle with my bare hands. Over the years, I have learned to embrace being a sissy.

There is no question that criticism has also hurt the church. We have to be careful what we say at home. There are little ears that don't miss a thing. I recall the time a member of our parish staff had a conflict with one of her volunteers. One morning that volunteer came into the parish office with her little daughter. The staff person, seeing the child, bent down and said, *"Hello, I'm Robin."* And the little tyke pulled back and said in surprise, *"You're Robin?"* as if looking up at the heartless Cruella of **101 Dalmatians**. Can you imagine what had been said about Robin in that child's home?

What have we said in front of our kids about our priest or the bishop or the church? And you wonder why your kids get negative attitudes about things religious? If parishioners, priests and staffs would stop criticizing one another and replace it with words of praise and thanks, some parishes would change overnight. There are ways to correct problems without going after people. If nothing else, and this is a minimum, we can, in the name of the love of children and church, at least be discreet in what we say and how we say it.

* * * * * * *

There is also little room for joy in a marriage, family or parish when **apathy** moves in. Apathy is not to be confused with laziness or with being tired. Apathy is giving up on someone we are supposed to love, a spouse, child or fellow parishioner. We resort to doing minimums. Just getting along, replaces intimacy. Being a good provider replaces being a real father. Meeting needs replaces real belonging. The tragedy of apathy is not just that it exposes the death of love for the other; it discourages the other person so much they will give up on themselves as well.

> After 35 years of marriage, a husband and wife came to counseling. When asked what the problem was, the wife went into a tirade listing every problem they had ever had over the years. On and on and on: neglect, lack of intimacy, emptiness, loneliness, feeling unloved and unlovable, an entire laundry list of unmet needs she had endured. Finally, after allowing this for a sufficient length of time, the therapist got up, walked around the desk, and after asking the wife to stand, he embraced her and kissed

her long and passionately as her husband watched - with a raised eyebrow. The woman settled down and quietly returned to her seat as though in a daze. The therapist then turned to the husband and said, *"This is what your wife needs at least three times a week. Can you do this?"* *"Well,"* the husband replied, *"I can drop her off here on Mondays and Wednesdays, but on Fridays, I fish."*

Now, that's apathy! There is no way such an attitude can inspire or give life. It is so empty it is like a vacuum that sucks life out of a marriage, not to mention a family. The issue is no longer us, but me. Apathetic people are particularly unattractive in that they run neither hot nor cold, and you want to gag. How in God's name can apathetic people teach the ways of love?

I was in a parish where a parishioner told me, *"You priests come and go. I'll be here long after you leave."* In other words, he would put up with me but not work with me. He had given up on me. He had written me off. Ironically, he moved away before I did. By the same token, when we priests give up on our people, we settle for providing services to insure the smooth operation of the parish, but withdraw from any personal investment as good shepherds of our flock. What has happened, of course, is that we succumbed to apathy, we gave up on love and we stopped growing. Of course, our parish probably stopped growing in love as well.

* * * * * * *

The first cousin to apathy is **irresponsibility**. I remember the old Eddie Fisher songs (in the 50's) about climbing the highest mountains and swimming the deepest oceans for one's sweetheart. In all too many marriages, there comes the time when the same guy won't change the littlest diaper or wash the smallest bowl for his wife. Those could be great acts of love! These are symptoms of someone's reneging on the shared responsibility of the marital relationship. When this happens, it is a clear sign that he is no longer invested in his wife nor is she in her husband.

Believe me, I wouldn't send anyone to such a home to see what *"loving one another as I have loved you"* looks like.

Are helping the kids with homework, going to PTA meetings, and disciplining the children tasks left to one spouse only? That's irresponsible. Love demands you share those responsibilities. Even if only one can attend a PTA meeting, the other needs to know what's going on so they can both take responsibility for the education of their children. It is also important to share the financial affairs of the home. I have seen all too often a widowed person lost when their spouse dies who had maintained total control in this area. Again, while one may do the actual work, sharing information is necessary. As humdrum as this may sound, love does such things. And we will never learn to love this way without trying it. Even in the most mundane dimensions of life, there are lessons of love to learn . . . and teach.

In the parish, it is love that demands that all the people share the responsibility for the spirit of the parish. We can't leave it just up to the priest, the staff or a handful of volunteers. What would happen to our parishes if all parishioners chose to accept their responsibility for the spirit of hospitality, joy and warmth in their parish, not to mention financial support? What would happen to our liturgies if everyone accepted their responsibility to enter fully into the prayer and singing? They would be transformed! Even the boring kids wouldn't be so bored anymore! Your parish might even get written up in the diocesan newspaper! In a family - and we constantly speak of the parish community as a "parish family" - this should happen.

* * * * * * *

The fifth indication that we are failing to embrace each other's brokenness is when **pride** raises its ugly head in the form of arrogance and independence. We're not talking here about the pride of sensing one's worth and dignity, but the first of the seven deadly cardinal sins kind of pride that makes people think they are the center of the universe. While independence is *the* great American virtue, it is nowhere touted as a virtue in the scriptures, for it is also an attack on the very heart of a committed relationship. It places *"me"* before *"us"* and *"my way"* above *"our way."* It makes unity impossible because it cannot embrace another opinion, idea, or suggestion with openness. When pride enters a relationship, we love another only on our own terms. We become very controlling. Rather than belonging to my beloved, I really belong only to myself. If someone were to sing Frank Sinatra's "I Did It My Way" at my funeral, thinking it expressed the best of my character, I'd consider myself to be in deep trouble.

We cannot love only on our own terms. It's impossible. Of its very nature, love is always looking out for what is best for one's beloved. *"Greater love than this no one has than to lay down one's life for one's friends."* When couples get married, they, in effect, say to each other, *"I pledge to love you in such a way that you will never ever have to question or doubt just how loved and lovable you are."* On their wedding day, that certainly is their heart's desire. Of course, they don't live up to that pledge. Nobody does. So love calls them to forgive and begin again, a pattern that will be repeated over and over in their marriage.

But before the forgiveness happens, we hope that all involved will try to learn from their sins, their mistakes, from their actions that caused so much hurt and pain in their family. After all, that is what redemption is all about. God's love does not just heal a hurt. It leads to growth as well. Our weakness and sinfulness are the givens. Facing them honestly is the first step toward a better future.

That is just how critical finding the way of love really is. Without it, they have no future. On a television news magazine type show, a marriage counselor was featured who had found the most amazing way to get couples to heal their broken relationships. His secret was talked about as though it were the then newly discovered genome. His secret? He got couples to forgive each other. This novel idea has been our Catholic tradition for two thousand years.

I firmly believe that the family is the most important school in the world for teaching the ways of love because, in the family, our couples are committed to love. That's why they got together in the first place. They loved each other. And because they love their kids so much, the kids will take them to places they don't want to go. And by the time they have raised them, the parents, not the kids, will have matured in love. The whole experience of raising a family constantly teaches them the ways of love. Granted, the kids learn to love as well, but the school of daily life in the home makes our married couples the real experts on the ways of love, not people with Ph.D.'s after their names. What I used to say on the Marriage Encounter weekend years ago is worth repeating, "If we can't turn to our sacramental couples to show us how to love, to whom do we turn?" Who else is committed to love as our couples are, even when they don't feel like it?

CONVERSATION STARTERS:

1. Why is love so critical to the human condition?

2. What makes the pain of love worthwhile to you?

3. In what ways may you be hindering the flow of love in your home?

4. What difference does your family make to our church and to our society?

5. What place does your faith play in this?

---

1. C.S. Lewis, The Four Loves (New York, NY: Harcourt, 1960), 123

2. Richard Rohr, Everything Belongs (Crossroads Publishing Company, New York), p. 50

3. Anthony J. Schulte, Weekday Homily Helps, (Anthony Messenger Press) 21 October 2009

4. Thomas L. Vandenberg, A Sign for Our Time, Pastoral and matrimonial Renewal Center, PO Box 2304, Southeastern, PA 19399-2304, 1982

CHAPTER FIVE

THE DEPTH AND BREADTH OF LOVE

"God wants us to be dance instructors."

A lawyer took his seat in the airplane next to an Irishman. He thought to himself that this guy would be a good mark, and he could have some fun with him. However, the Irishman was tired and just wanted to sleep. After failed efforts at starting a conversation, the lawyer said, *"Let's play a game."* The Irishman didn't respond. So he persisted, *"It will be fun. I ask you a question, and if you don't know the answer, you give me five dollars. Then you ask me a question, and if I don't know the answer, I'll give you $500."* Well, this got the Irishman's attention.

The lawyer asked, *"What is the distance between the earth and the moon?"* Without saying a word, the Irishman sleepily reached into his pocket and pulled out a five dollar bill and handed it to the lawyer, then he started to doze off once again. *You get to ask me a question now,"* the lawyer said. Opening one eye, the Irishman asked, *"What has three legs when it goes up hill and four legs when it comes down?"* Then he closed his eyes.

While he slept, the lawyer digs out his laptop and *Google's* everything he can think of that might reveal the answer. Frustrated after an hour of searching, he gives up, shakes the Irishman and hands him $500, who takes it and goes back to sleep. *"You can't go to sleep,"* the lawyer pleads, *"I need to know the answer. What goes up a hill with three legs and comes down with four?"* The Irishman reaches into his pocket and pulls out another five dollar bill and gives it to the lawyer.

* * * * * * *

It is never wise to take people for granted, especially if we think we are somehow superior to them. We are just opening ourselves up for some unpleasant surprises. This chapter will deal with some of those unpleasant surprises. What we say here will be a good example of how the Sacrament of Matrimony has something important to say to the church-at-large. Our couples have more to say than we may think, and, for that matter, more than even they may think. At this particular time in our church, we just may need to listen to what they have to say more than ever. As the importance of this extraordinary sacrament became clearer to me, and I could see it held even more surprises.

I'll get to the reason I say this in a moment, but one more very important thing needs to be said first. The two social sacraments of the church, Orders and Matrimony, are both necessary for the life and proper functioning of the church. Rather than being in competition, as we indicated earlier, they are meant to work together, the one encouraging and reinforcing the other. Each emphasizes a dimension of Christ's love that is crucial if the church is to be a true sacrament of Christ to the world.

On the one hand, our sacramental couples commit to a depth of love that is unwavering and even profound. Like Jesus' love, there is nothing superficial or artificial about it. On the other hand, priests have a love for the church that is broad and all embracing. It mirrors the love of Jesus that is truly all inclusive. In the role of pastor, a priest reaches out to the whole parish community; no one is excluded from his pastoral concerns. These two dimensions of love together mirror and make real the depth and breadth of Christ's love. These two social sacraments compliment each other, teaming up, as it were, to call the church to a way of life that is truly Christ-like.

On their wedding day and afterwards, the priest, on behalf of the believing community, not only calls the couple to a depth of love for each other, but also a breadth of love that extends beyond them. He reminds them that their love is like that lamp that is meant to give light to all in the house. He is there to help them remember this call as time goes by, and to encourage them to spend their love for others, beginning with their children.

And it is the role of our sacramental couples to call their priests to a depth of love so they will more fully image Christ's love to the people they serve. This underscores the need of the priest to have a genuine relationship with his people, not just a shallow or superficial one. While this depth of relationship is very difficult to pull off in our huge parishes, it is to be expected that the priest will always treat his people with loving respect. Rather than speak down to them, he will show his care and compassion for them, especially during the important events in their lives, like at baptisms, weddings, funerals and at times of illness and misfortune. Our couples call priests to a depth of love, while our priests call the couples to a breadth of love.

Visually, as you bring the vertical line of depth and the horizontal line of breadth together, they form a cross (✝), the symbol of the depth of Jesus' love for all people. Working in cooperation as social sacraments, our priests and couples help each other to enable the church to make the fullness of Christ's love real in the world. As partners, they call the whole church to a depth and breadth of love as the sacrament of Christ for the world.

* * * * * * *

Now, why did I say the church needs our sacramental couples today more than ever? It is because we have just come through the greatest scandal to ever hit the Catholic Church in the United States, and our couples can help us understand how it happened as well as show us a way to healing. The truth is the scandal's aftershocks continue to shake the ecclesial ground under our feet. The most damaging part of the scandal was not that some priests were active pedophiles and repeatedly abused numbers of children, although that would have been plenty enough scandal by itself. But, at least, that could have been explained as an example of fallen human nature and human weakness.

Sadly, the subsequent scandal that caused the most damage to the church, the one that led to the bankruptcy of some dioceses, was the failure of some bishops to protect children under their care by transferring known abusive priests from one parish to another where they could continue their abusive behavior. That is much harder to understand, considering what we know today about the nature of pedophilia and its apparent formidable resistance to cure.

However, it is important to remember that 30 and 40 years ago, when much of the known abuse first began, even those in the mental health professions didn't understand the seriousness of this predatory behavior as it raised its ugly head in the church and elsewhere. Mistakenly, many bishops trusted that the professionals knew what they were doing and thought that their priests could be rehabilitated and thus return to ministry as a danger to no one. Although they were acting in good faith, it was a tragic error, as many bishops will now admit.

But once the serious nature of this pathology became clear, any such subsequent personnel moves were inexcusable, and some happened. If those transfers had not been made, the initial scandal would have died an ignominious death without ever building up a head of steam. Furthermore, the church's truly extraordinary measures that were then developed to insure the safety of our children by keeping pedophiles out of the priesthood and ministerial positions in the church would have been seen for what they are, a model for the rest of society to follow.

My purpose here is not to rehash the scandal, but to focus on what our sacramental couples might have to offer in bringing some insight and healing to the church. Ironically, I believe that our married couples, so violated by the institution when their concerns were ignored, have a significant role to play in the healing and in the restoration of the church's public image. Why? Because they point us to that kind of love Jesus commanded that we have for one another, that deep, laying-down-of-one's-life kind of love. From the little things couples do each day to the major decisions they have to make, they are guided by Jesus' words, *"Love one another as I have loved you" (John 13:34).* These same words should have guided the institution's response to the scandal when it broke.

Our people want to believe in their priests and bishops. Priests and bishops should want to believe in their people just as much, and in this case, especially our sacramental couples. Yet, they didn't. In many cases, the parents of abused children were seen as a threat, almost as enemies of the church, or at least as unimportant. They were not prepared for this kind of treatment. They can accept our mistakes, our being wrong, and even our sins, but, for many, their faith was so formed that they truly expected to find love at work in us no matter what. But it was not there, and some good people simply walked away. Others drifted in and out. Some remained only because they don't know where else to go. Yet, in spite of it all, the vast majority remained in the church because they still trust it has the words of everlasting life.

To me, it is amazing how much our people believed in us! Now, if those in authority had had a similar faith in the goodness of the parents who realized that their child was abused by a priest, especially since they were sacraments of the church, the bishops would have had second thoughts about being suspicious of them or as seeing them as potential enemies of the institutional church. And yet, as I recall stories that came to light in various parts of our country, the manner of treatment some parents received might even be considered sacrilegious.

I have friends in California whose son was abused by a priest. They were told by the ecclesial authorities to be quiet, like nothing had happened, lest bad publicity come to the church and priest. They were told to dismiss the incident and not make waves, implying that what had happened was unimportant because they were unimportant. It hurt them deeply and resulted in their serious disillusionment with the church which they had served most generously over the years. What bothered them the most was the implication that their son was unimportant. Parental instincts then took over as they said to themselves, *"You can hurt us, we can take it, but when it comes to hurting our baby, that's another story!"* They felt marginalized, even ostracized by the Church, forget about being believed in as a sacrament. Sacrilegious? You make the call.

My point here is not to be overly critical of anyone, even the bishops, but to show that we all need to have a greater respect for the Sacrament of Matrimony. When the scandal broke, I'm sure this thought never even entered anyone's head. Yet, it would have carried more weight than the advice some bishops apparently received from their legal counsel. From what I've read, it seems that it was only the threat of litigation that changed the behavior of some bishops. No one should have been surprised when parents became angry once they learned that their own church leaders did not support their passion to do everything they could to keep their children safe. By divine plan, parents will instinctively do all they can to protect their children, and, sadly, this truth was not honored.

The problem for celibate priests and bishops is that we really do not know the depth of love that parents have for their children since we never experienced it. That kind of love can only be learned from the "inside." Had those in leadership positions in the church known that kind of love, I am confident the initial abuse scandal would have been handled much differently. But they didn't know. Consequently, in too many cases our couples' genuine concerns were simply dismissed. This is a good example of why believing in our couples must be an important dimension of our Catholic way of life. We as a church must learn from our mistakes.

Among the many things that this tragic story teaches us is the importance of our couple's vocation as living sacraments of the church to call the clergy, priests and bishops alike, to a depth of love for their people that reflects the depth of love that Jesus has for us; a depth of love reflected by parents' love for their children. Again, while we call our couples to a breadth of love, they call us to a depth of love. We who are the clergy of the church are not dispensed from loving deeply, especially those little ones who love and trust us so very much. Through the Sacrament of Matrimony, our couples call us to a real depth of love in our relationships. This may be another surprise we didn't expect to hear. After all, who ever thought our married couples could have something so important to offer the clergy?

Through ignorance more than arrogance we have ignored our couples and their identity as living sacraments of the church, precious living gems, pearls of great price, in the church's rich treasury. It never dawned on most of us that our couples not only needed us to believe in them but also that we, for our own good, needed to believe in them as well. While there are many things our couples do need and want from us, one of the most important is our faith in them as living sacraments. Like the woman in the gospel story who would gratefully eat crumbs that fell from the master's table and thereby gain Jesus' respect *(Matt. 15:21)*, so too do our married couples deserve our respect. Like that woman, so many of our couples are people of great faith.

More than anyone else I know, our sacramental couples are committed to a way of life that mirrors that kind of self-giving, self-sacrificing love that Jesus lived. Day in and day out, their vocation is to remind the church and us of that high standard. Jesus died for us so we could live. Parents will die for their children so they can live. I know husbands who will die so their wives can live, and wives who spend their lives so their husbands can live. There is no greater kind of love. This reminds me of a story.

A teacher observed that one of the little boys in her class was pensive and withdrawn. *"What are you worried about?"* she asked. *"My parents,"* he replied. *"Dad works all day to keep me clothed and fed and sends me to the best school in town. And he's working overtime to be able to send me to college. Mom spends all day cooking and cleaning and ironing and shopping so I have nothing to worry about."* *"Why, then, are you worried?"* the teacher asked. *"I'm afraid they might try to escape."*

* * * * * * *

But there is more. Love without power is sentimentality. Power without love is tyranny. However, when power and love work together, we have something that gives life and gives it in abundance. We have credibility. When blended together in a couple's relationship, power and love compose the force behind the Sacrament of Matrimony. It is expressed most obviously in a couple's role as parents, but it is in no way limited to that or to things that happen in the home.

Interestingly, since love and power combined are also the essential qualities of a true leader, especially in the church, we see again how our couples have something terribly important to offer their priests and even their bishops: the qualities that make up a true and effective servant leader. Yes, Jesus gave Peter the keys of the kingdom. But before commissioning Peter to begin his ministry as head of the church, Jesus asked him three times, *"Do you love me?" "Do you love me?" "Do you love me?"* This is more than a touching story of the healing of Peter's triple denial, for without love there is no way Peter could lead the church as the first pope, at least not in the spirit of Jesus.

There is no doubt that Jesus commissioned the church to teach, and to do so with authority. *"Go, therefore, and make disciples of all nations, baptizing them in the name of the Father, and of the Son, and of the Holy Spirit, teaching them to observe all that I have commanded you" (Matt. 28:19-20).* We took it seriously. And by golly, we taught what Jesus taught, and we did it with divine authorization knowing that we were right. Unfortunately and tragically, we even went so far as to say that error had no rights, and we got ourselves into terrible messes like the Inquisition when we mercilessly executed people who disagreed with us. The trouble isn't that we tried to teach the truth as we saw it, but the way we went about it. What was missing was the Spirit of Jesus in the way we taught. We must teach the truth in love. We must do the truth with love. And if we take the time to notice, we'll see couples living this way, before our very eyes, to remind us of this each day. I said the Sacrament of Matrimony was surprising.

What I am trying to say is that the special gift our sacramental couples bring to the church is that they show us how we are to live as the People of God: clergy, laity, bishops, priests, deacons, religious and people in the pew. They keep reminding us what is most important in life: the quality of our relationships with one another in Christ. They help us keep our priorities straight. And if we follow their lead, those who fill the leadership roles in the Church will live their lives in the Spirit of Jesus, in the Spirit of Love.

The authority that makes for a great leader, bishop or priest, comes from the quality of relationship he has, not only with God, but also with God's people. Granted, his position gives him authority, but that is from the "outside," external, as it were. He also needs authority that comes from within him as a human being. What impressed the centurion in the gospel was that Jesus would say, *"Come,"* and people came; *"Go"* and they went. Jesus had an inner authority that came from his relationship with his Father and with his people. He never acted alone. Jesus' power was effective because he exercised it *with* his disciples not *over* his disciples. That is why it worked. The Spirit connected them to one another. Effective leaders in the church will lead out of the Spirit of Jesus, the Spirit of God's love. And if they don't, their little part of the church, the Body of Christ, will be at risk, being sick, dying or dead.

You see, if some other spirit drives the institution, some spirit that does not come from the flow of grace in the church, that is the love relationship between its members, the church will, at best, be an unclear sign, a dubious sacrament of Christ to the world. What kind of relationship then, can it possibly have with those outside the church? That is another part of the scandal we are trying to overcome today. The church will always look bad when any of its prominent leaders, who should know better, lose touch with the Spirit that unites us and gives us life. The prayer of Jesus at the Last Supper needs to be on our lips everyday. *"May they be one Father as you are in me and I am in you. May they be one in us so the world may believe you sent me" (John 17:21).* What will make the church truly believable is not that it is *right* all the time, but that it is *loving* all the time. It must be committed to doing the truth in love.

* * * * * * *

To follow the way of love, to follow the way of Jesus is not always easy and will eventually lead to the cross in one way or the other. While our young married couples just want to share the gift of life with someone they love, they are, by the nature of their vocation as baptized Christians, a part of something far bigger than themselves. And the contribution they make to the church and society when living their commitment to love in the Spirit of Jesus is inestimable. Maybe they wish it were otherwise, but it isn't. As we say in the wedding ceremony, *"What God has joined ..."* This new union of husband and wife clearly fits into God's plan for humanity. Sometimes, its influences are subtle but still necessary.

It seems to me that Jesus' words in Matthew's Gospel speak to these couples in a special way, *"Take my yoke upon your shoulders and learn from me for I am gentle and humble of heart"* (Matt. 11:29). During the years of sharing the gift of life together, they learn their place in God's plan. They discover that their real joy in life and their power as a couple come from the love that goes back and forth between them as husband and wife. They discover that there is never a place for domination one over the other, as they will quickly realize that that isn't the way love works. They adjust accordingly as they learn from experience the paradoxical *"light burden"* of the way of love.

Marriage is the great equalizer. Even the powerful corporate executive comes home from an office where people coddle him, defer to him, and respect his privacy all day long, only to hear his wife say to him as he comes through the door at the end of the day, *"Honey, I sure am glad you're home. Would you please fix the leaking toilet upstairs when you have a chance?"* In an instant he is brought back to reality, and rightly so. Love does such things, and it's not really a burden.

Unfortunately, we priests don't have that built in "reality check" when we come home. Because our people treat us with such respect 24/7 we can get spoiled. Most parishioners are hesitant to "impose" upon us in any way, as though we are above it all, like we are on a pedestal of some sort.

Well, I've been around long enough to have seen priests on pedestals, and we don't look good there. It's not a healthy image to have for a priest. If we priests begin to think that our heads are so important that they will be properly adorned only with a biretta, we need to stop and reevaluate what it's all about.

Our couples remind us that when love is the thread that runs though all of our relationships, we can be expected to be "humbled" by the realities of life. And if we begin to think we should be treated with privilege, I recommend we go spend some time with a family to be reminded of what love looks like on a minute to minute basis. Again, if we can't turn to our couples who are committed to love each other as a way of life to show us this, to whom can we turn?

Someone needs to guide the church out of the malaise in which we currently find ourselves as a result of the abuse scandal. And the way out has to be consistent with the gospel. It has to be the way of love. More than anyone I know, our couples make love real, not just a nice idea or a gospel value. In a thousand different ways, they can teach us the steps of the dance of love. This is an awareness we need to rediscover.

If you don't mind my using some religious language here, as it serves as segue to the next chapter, I would say that there is something very prophetic about those called to the Sacrament of Matrimony. A prophet, you see, is not someone who foretells the future. Biblically, a prophet is one who sees clearly the reality of <u>now</u> and how what is happening now fits or doesn't fit into God's plan. By looking at our married couples who are living God's plan, who are living up to their vocation as sacraments of the church, we have a measurable standard of how the church is either living or not living God's plan today.

You see, the Sacrament of Matrimony exists, not in the husband or in the wife, but in space between them, in their relationship, in the dynamic of life that goes on back and forth connecting them one to the other. That is where the power is. That is where the energy is. That is where the grace is, the love of Jesus intertwined with their love. It is meant to be living, generative and healing. While the couple relationship is personal and private, it also calls for them as a couple to face outward together to those who need to see and learn from their love. And since they image the love of Jesus and bring it to bear on the events of life in the church today, at the heart of their prophetic role is the way they love. Clearly, their love isn't just for them. It is for us, all of us. It should be the standard against which we measure the vibrancy of the church, the People of God. Surprise!

CONVERSATION STARTERS:

1. As a social sacrament, why is the Sacrament of Matrimony so important?

2. Does this change the way you look at your marriage?

3. How do you call the people of the church to the depth of love?

4. How may you call the clergy to a depth of love?

5. In what way does this influence your life as a married couple?

CHAPTER SIX

A PROPHETIC VOICE

"Are you sure it wasn't a wrong number?"

The first Sunday in the parish, the new pastor gave a wonderful homily. Everyone was thrilled. He was articulate and his voice was strong, his message clear and he delivered it with just the right amount of reverence, authority, sensitivity and enthusiasm. He used inflection, humor and a varied tempo appropriate to his words. The congregation was spellbound. After Mass, people leaving church made it a point to tell him how much they appreciated his wonderful homily.

The next Sunday, to the surprise of everyone, he delivered exactly the same homily, with the same words, gestures, inflections and tempo. The people were a bit confused but said nothing, figuring he had just forgotten he had delivered the same homily the week before. After all, it had been a busy week. They thanked him again as they left church.

The next Sunday, he delivered the exact same homily for the third week in a row, again with the same words, gestures, inflections and tempo. Most people just walked by him after Mass not knowing what to say. However, as there is in every parish, a woman came up to him and said,

"Father, that was a good homily and all, but why did you give it again; you've delivered exactly the same homily for three weeks straight? What's the matter, don't you know anything else?" "Well," the priest said to her, *"you haven't done anything about this one yet."*

* * * * * * *

Something may be good, informative and even inspiring, but if we don't act on it what's the point? To some people, I made what may seem to be an outlandish claim in that last chapter, stating that our sacramental couples have a prophetic role to play in the church. If that is true, as I think we may just be discovering, we should look carefully at acting on it. Granted, our couples don't think that way, and that's perfectly all right. In fact, it may be good they don't. After all, what they have to say by their lives may not be what people want to hear. This chapter will look at how this may be. Again, it calls us to change the way we look at the Sacrament of Matrimony.

Few prophets worth their salt ever wanted to be one, let alone think they were one. But as living sacraments of Christ's love present in the community of faith, we would surely expect our couples to *"let their light shine before others, that seeing their works, they may give praise to their Father in heaven" (Matt:5:16)*. We need to pay attention and act on what we see! By the way, this makes it clear that we are not on this earth to get to heaven, although it is certainly a worthy goal to have. More importantly, we are here to give glory to God by building the kingdom! If we live to do that, the getting to heaven part will take care of itself. Well, anyway…

At times, a sacramental couple's very presence in the community may have something to say to us either directly or indirectly. They don't say it from the pulpit, but by the way they live with one another and how they express the values they place on their relationships in the normal events of daily life. Knowing this, it is reasonable that we should look to our sacramental couples and how they deal with issues in their lives to help us deal with some of the issues in ours, particularly those issues that impact our relationships; above all, the relationships we have with one another as members of the church. In fact, I think we would be remiss not to.

Bishop Robert Morneau of Green Bay, Wisconsin said something to a gathering of our priests several years ago that has been very helpful to me. He said, *"The main thing is to know the main thing and to keep the main thing the main thing."* If I'm driving a car, the main thing is to get to my destination safely. That should influence the way I drive the whole journey. As followers of Jesus the main thing is the nature and quality of the relationship we have with one another and with God. (This is what gives glory to God.) In other words, what is going on between us? Is it life-giving or not; a movement toward freedom, justice and peace or not? In short, is it an expression of love or not? We take our cue from St. Paul. *"If I give away all that I possess, piece by piece, and if I even let them take my body to burn it, but am without love, it will do me no good whatever"* (1 Cor. 13:3). Clearly, for St. Paul the main thing is love. We need to know this and we need to remember this and we need to act on this.

A friend of mine maintains that the two main causes of tension in a marriage are money and sex. This must be before the kids turn 15, but I'll take his words as true. Therefore, in a marriage, even though a couple may argue about money and sex, the real issue is neither money nor sex; it is what money and sex are doing to the couple's relationship. That's the ultimate issue. It's not how much time one spends on the job, but what that time on the job is doing to their relationship or to their relationship with the kids. The main thing is the flow of love going on between the couple and between the family members. When a couple is living the grace of the Sacrament of Matrimony, their relationship of love is clearly the main thing. And that is what *"gives light to all in the house."*

Another friend of mine tells of the time she went with her husband to a company sponsored retreat at an up-scale resort in Florida. When she was alone, some vice presidents of the company started to lean on her so she would encourage her husband to accept a vice presidential role in the company also. They assured her that it would mean a big jump in salary and great perks like other retreat weekends at similar luxurious resorts and so forth. Knowing who the men were, she asked one them, *"Are you married?" "I was,"* he said, *"but we divorced a while back."* She asked another, and he was divorced also; and a third, the same thing, divorced. Then she said to them, *"Do you think I am going to encourage my husband to take the same job you have so he can be like you?"* She wasn't a fool. She was a wife, and her relationship with her husband was the main thing.

We should measure what is going on in the church, relationship-wise, by that standard, for it is no less important. Look at what has happened to the church as a result of the abuse scandal. Its public image has been severely damaged. We priests became the brunt of jokes on late night television. At its height, some priests I know hesitated to wear their clerical collars in public because they feared that people would be suspicious of them; others began to keep all children at arm's length. I wrestled with this as well, but made a decision to wear my clericals when I normally would have and let the little ones hug my kneecaps. I was no pedophile, and I refused to let the priesthood be defined by the few in the presbyterate who were. How sad that the popular media kept this scandal before the public eye in such a way as to imply that it might be what the Catholic priesthood was all about. We were all painted with the same tainted brush that was just as hurtful and unjust as any racial or ethnic slur.

But the situation within the church is no better. For instance, I know some wonderful people who have left the church over it. Others, deeply discouraged and disillusioned have pulled back from church involvement and support. Many of us are angry, certainly at the abusers, and even at some bishops. Unfortunately, the Dallas Charter, which the bishops of the United States issued in 2002 to address the scandal, has apparently stopped the bleeding, but it hasn't brought healing. Consequently, the primary issue that we now need to address is no longer the child abuse scandal at all, nor even the bishops' response to it, good or bad. It is the quality of our relationships with one another in the church and how it has been affected by the abuse scandal. Only when that is clear can proper action be taken.

The relationship between some priests and bishops is strained. The discipline of priests throughout America has clearly tightened. We priests know that we could be just one accusation away from being stripped of our priestly ministry, not to mention our good name. We fear we will be presumed guilty rather than innocent. Many priests around the country (along with lay ecclesial ministers) already removed from ministry feel betrayed by the church as expendable, regardless of decades of faithful service. Some priests have also been subsequently shunned by their dioceses over some boundary violation that happened years before, even though they are neither pedophiles nor a present danger to anyone today. This tension that exists between some priests and their bishops should be a major concern as it has become a morale issue for many. Remember, the issue isn't who's right, or even the fear of a future lawsuit. It's the quality of our relationship with one another. It is not good.

As I write this, I feel uneasy, especially since many of our lay people have no idea that these tensions even exist. But some know. As one man in his 80's who is very aware of the national scene said to me, *"This is a real challenge to my faith."* And most priests know. But in a family where tensions exist, even though only a few other family members may know what is going on, that family would be considered dysfunctional if it didn't address them. I am sure that countless couples have resolved serious issues between themselves that their children never suspected in any way. To me, addressing the need to resolve the tensions in the church is too important to pass over like they didn't exist, as unpleasant as it is to admit them. But to ignore them would be like living with our heads in the sand. Healing won't be possible unless the pain is addressed. What's the point of moving on to other issues if we haven't done anything about this one first?

Am I overstating the problem? I hope so. But, as any responsible married couple will say, *"If we even suspect there may be a problem in our relationship, we need to address it. We can't pretend it is not there."* The same is true for the church. Unless all priests and bishops find a way to improve the quality of their relationship with one another, I don't see how they can be a believable sign of God's love and mercy to the rest of the church; forget the world! The good name of the Church has been hurt enough already. We need to come to believe in one another again, and it goes both ways. Until we do, we are restricting the flow of divine love in the church, thus making it harder to be seen as believable. And that goes to the very heart of our identity as a church and the reason the church exists!

How all of this is to be done is not my issue here. But our sacramental couples do have lived experiences that can teach us. That is their prophetic role. Married couples know what it is to have tension in their homes, between themselves as husbands and wives and with other members of the family. They know embarrassment, disappointment and discouragement. An alcoholic spouse can tear a family apart, as can a teen who has gotten involved in the drug culture. There are few experiences more painful for a family than to see one's parent or one's child go to jail. It is devastating.

But there is one thing they never do when there is love in the home. They never write off that family member. Some may leave home and never intend to return, but they know that if they change their mind, the odds are very much in their favor that they will be welcomed back. As Robert Frost said, *"Home is a place where, when you have to go there, they have to take you in."* As humiliating as the situation may be, she is still a mother, daughter or sister; he is still a father, son or brother. Because it is a family relationship it cannot be ignored. And should a family member become destructive to other family members, that person may be asked not to come home as a last resort, but he/she will always be remembered, loved and in the family's prayers.

* * * * * * *

I find the metaphor of the church as a family very helpful, while some people are not comfortable with the notion of the church as family at all. As a metaphor it falls short. That's okay by me. After all, all metaphors fall short when we try to understand the mystery of the divine. But the image of a family can help us understand something of the mystery of the church. Besides, the church as family has a rich tradition. In Eucharistic Prayer III, the church herself uses this metaphor: *"Listen graciously to the prayers of this family, whom you have summoned before you."* And in Eucharistic Prayer II we pray, *"Remember also our brothers and sisters who have fallen asleep . . ."*

In Mark's account of the gospel, we can't forget the time Jesus' family came looking for him. Jesus is told, *"Your mother, brothers and sisters are outside asking for you."* He replied, *". . . Anyone who does the will of God, that person is my brother and sister and mother."* In other words, Jesus takes the meaning of family to a whole new, even profound level. Rather than shy away from his relationship with his followers as familial, he affirms and deepens it. He calls for a relationship of intimacy that is born of faith not of blood. Family resemblances are not in terms of sharing common physical characteristics like eyes, nose and gait, but in the sharing of common spiritual characteristics like compassion, forgiveness, integrity, peacefulness and love. They are our family traits as Catholic Christians; at least they should be.

In fact, this relationship of intimacy is crucial to the proclamation of the gospel. *"May they be one, Father, as you are in me and I am in you; may they be one in us <u>so the world may believe</u> you sent me"* (John 17:21). If the church is not a family, or if the use of "family" causes more harm than good, then we should stop using the word and all references to our familial relationships with others in the church that say it is. But in the light of Jesus' words, I don't see how we can.

Actually, there is an interesting evolution of how Jesus addresses those who were close to him. First, they were just followers, then disciples, then servants, then friends; but after the resurrection Jesus called them brothers and sisters. Maybe the problem with calling the church a family is that that just isn't our experience. When I was a young boy, I recall the time I greeted a visiting priest to our parish by saying, *"Good morning."* He answered me in a stern, condescending voice with considerable irritation, *"You mean, 'Good morning Father.'"* He sure didn't express the demeanor of any father I had ever known. Furthermore, thinking of the church as a family does call for a level of commitment and intimacy that simply makes some of us feel uncomfortable.

It is important that we know what love looks like in a family, whether it be of the home or the church. In times of joy, it looks bright, happy, secure, warm and peaceful. It wears a smile, sleeps soundly and has inner feelings of well-being. But family life is not always joyful and happy.

Things go wrong; we hurt one another and let each other down. At these times, love may look sad. It may look shocked. It may even look uncaring. Love for a wayward child brings tears that stream down a mother's face, or long nights to a pastor who can't sleep. That's what love can look like. And that is why it all hurts so much. There are only two options to stop the pain of it all. Either we stop loving or we find a way to heal the hurt. However, the one thing we can't afford to lose in the home or church during these trying times is the love we are commanded to have for one another. To love at such times may be the most difficult thing we will ever have to do, but I see no other way that is compatible with the gospel of Jesus.

Our couples remind us that when we argue about the latest liturgical changes, the real issue is how these changes are affecting our relationships with one another in the church, at the parish, diocesan and even the universal levels, not to mention our relationship with God. What are those changes doing to us? Are we becoming polarized, breaking up into camps? Are we beginning to regard those who disagree with us as enemies? Do we stop talking to one another? In other words, what effect is it having on the flow of love between us? I believe we need to ask these kinds of questions. Of course, according to Jesus, there is no excuse for our not loving one another!

If we think this is pushing this "love stuff" too far, remember how Jesus himself put it: *"By this love you have for one another, everyone will know that you are my disciples" (John 13:35).* This is an example of our family resemblance. As any couple committed to their relationship can teach us, in a fight, when one loses, they both lose. They do not fight to defeat the other, but for the sake of their relationship. That's the main thing. The gospel is not about us vs. them, but us together … all of us. If this is being too idealistic, so be it. It at least keeps us on target, and being off target, missing the mark, is the meaning of sin.

* * * * * * *

What we observe in our couples will not be earthshaking or even prophetic most of the time, but their constant presence in our lives will help us be aware of the primacy of our relationships when we try to live out the gospel message from day to day. We should be able to see what genuine Christ-like love looks like. And we should be able to measure how well we are living as the People of God by holding our couples up as the standard. Again, you may say this is an overstatement. Maybe so, but the Catholic Catechism says that I am, by the Sacrament of Orders, an *alter Christus*, another Christ. Knowing myself as I do, that sounds like an overstatement, too. But the real issue is how being an *altar Christus* affects my relationship with my people. That's the main thing. So, let's look more closely at how this works, especially priests, as it might influence the way we understand the nature of the vocation to priesthood and role of the priest as "father" in the Catholic family.

Granted, some will stress the idea that an ontological change happens to a man when he receives the Sacrament of Orders, that is to say, that somehow his very being changes, that he becomes somehow unique, more to the likeness of Christ's being. I don't argue with this, but at a very practical level, I am very aware that my ordination to the priesthood didn't change my feet. They are still made of clay. I'll never measure up. Yet, that lofty image is held out to us priests. Why, then, is it not appropriate to hold out to our couples the image of Christ's love for them to make real in our lives, ontological change or not? If the priest makes the power of Jesus present in the church real to the people he serves, so too, do our sacramental couples make the love of Jesus real to the people they serve. Remember, sacraments confer what they signify.

For the sake of conversation, let's accept that I am an *alter Christus*. The Catechism of the Catholic Church uses this concept around the power a priest has to act in the person of Christ (#1552). It does not mean that I am to see myself as a cut above the laity; that I deserve to be on that pedestal, and others should do me homage. No. Such a pompous attitude just opens the door to the dangers of a clericalism that serves only to separate a priest from his people. That can't be what it means. Being a priest is not about the priest. To be an *alter Christus* should not affect my hat size, but my heart size. It means that I am to have a heart that reflects the heart of Christ and to love the way Christ loves. If it puffs up my ego, it could be distorted into something that fights the very way of life Jesus calls me to live. Jesus was not about Jesus. Jesus was about the Father and us. He was obedient to his Father by loving us to the end. Rather than above us, he was *"in our midst as one who serves us"* (Luke 22:27).

> A famous movie star went to a nursing home to entertain the residents. Being aware of his celebrity status, he was surprised that no one seemed excited to see him. A bit miffed, he asked, *"Does anyone here know who I am?"* An elderly woman pointed to a nurse sitting behind a desk and said, *"Go ask her. She'll tell you."*

For me, the *alter Christus* image that comes to mind is not Jesus standing on a pedestal. (The cross is the closest thing to a pedestal he was ever on.) Furthermore, Jesus didn't make his triumphal entry into Jerusalem on a stallion, but a donkey. Therefore, the image I have of being an *alter Christus* is Jesus on his knees washing the feet of his disciples. Now, as sacraments of Christ's love, and to reinforce that image of service, I turn to our couples to show me what self-giving love looks like. It's their prophetic role in the church because their love isn't just for them. It is also for us. As parents, practically their whole existence is about feeding the hungry, clothing the naked, caring for the sick and washing behind their kids' ears.

Let me say one more word about this. The significance of what happened to me the day the bishop imposed his hands on my head and conferred on me the Sacrament of Orders was not so much that I changed ontologically somehow, (which I don't deny) but rather that my relationship with the People of God changed dramatically, even profoundly. The way I see it, Jesus gave his power to the Church, and we priests give voice to the presence of Jesus in the Church. The Church is also an *altar Christus*, for in baptism, we all *"put on Christ,"* Jew, Greek, slave, free, male and female (Galatians 3:27).

To say the church is the Body of Christ is more than a simple metaphor. At the time of Saul's conversion experience, when he was persecuting the Christians, the voice he heard said, *"Saul, Saul, why do you persecute me"* (Acts 9:4)*?* He asked who was speaking and the voice said, *"I am Jesus you are persecuting."* From this experience, St. Paul developed his idea of the church as the Body of Christ. As I say, it is more than a metaphor. We priests make the church present when we celebrate the sacraments, or speak on its behalf. The priest could also be seen as the *altar ecclesia,* or more accurately*,* as one who acts *"in persona ecclesiae."* Because of the unique relationship he has with the bishop as head of the local church, he acts "in the person of the church."

This is certainly implied in the ritual for Anointing of the Sick. While St. James speaks of the practice of calling for the priests of the church to anoint the sick with oil (James 5:14), the prayer of thanksgiving for the oil just before the actual anointing takes place says, *"God of mercy, ease the suffering and comfort the weakness of your servant N., whom <u>the Church anoints</u> with this holy oil."* It is like the whole parish is gathered at the bedside of the sick person. The priest is no longer mentioned. Note also that in the Sacrament of Reconciliation, when we grant absolution we say, *"Through the <u>ministry of the Church</u>, may God grant you pardon and peace."* While the priest says, *"I forgive you from your sins ..."* he is speaking on behalf of the Church enlivened by the Spirit of the compassionate Jesus present in the Church. The same is true when he says the words of institution at Mass, *"This is my Body."* He speaks with the power of Jesus present in the assembly gathered around him.

At a practical level, it seems to me that we priests draw our "power" from the church because of our unique relationship with the church, the People of God who called us to Orders through the ministry of the bishop. If this is true, and I believe it is, then it underscores the need that we priests have for a strong and healthy relationship with the church, meaning the People of God, beginning with our bishops.

When a bishop removes a priest from ministry, it simply means that he breaks the official relationship of the priest with the People of God. Even if he still has certain powers since he is a "priest forever," he can no longer legitimately exercise them on behalf of the church. The only exception is in an emergency situation when someone is dying. In fact, the church herself supplies the faculties to such a priest in this specific case so he can hear that person's confession. It is an example of the compassion of Christ present in the church. Again, the proper exercise of a priest's power is linked to the relationship he has in faith with the People of God.

While the priest acts with the power of Christ, and lest he gets too enamored by this truth of faith, it is the Sacrament of Matrimony that serves as a constant reminder for him to exercise that power in a spirit of love. He uses his power as priest for the sake of strengthening the life of the community he serves, never to serve himself or anything else aside from his people. Power and love seem to need each other if they are to transform the faith community into the likeness of Jesus.

In light of this, I can't help but wonder how things would have been if those bishops who knowingly transferred abusive priests to new assignments had focused their concern primarily on their relationship with their people rather than on protecting their position of power or the image of the institutional church. What if they had acted on their role as an *alter Christus*, another Christ, as primarily a servant to their people, looking up to them as one must when washing feet? Or better yet, what if they had acted *in persona ecclesiae*, that is, in the person of the church, the People of God? What would have happened if they had realized that the depth of the self-giving love that parents had for their abused children was the depth of love they were meant to have had for them as well? Quite frankly, had that happened, I can't imagine the culpable transfer of an abusive priest ever happening. Certainly, things would have been very different. *"If"* is truly a little word with a big meaning.

* * * * * * *

For the sake of clarity, maybe this is the place where we need to do some defining of words, especially the word love. We've been told the Eskimos have a hundred words for snow, and we just assumed it was true. However, I recently heard that this is just a popular myth. But really, it doesn't matter. God only knows how many words there are for love in

English, but there are four in Greek, and I'm sticking with these four. Each word reveals something about this mysterious experience, and may even point us in the direction of the One who is Love.

The first is *storge* love. This is a "feel good" kind of love, a love of abiding affection. It is the way a mother feels when she rocks her baby, or the way a baby feels when being rocked. Without receiving this *storge* love, a baby can be emotionally damaged for life or even die. It seems to open the door to deeper forms of love. Storge love in its most simple form is at work when we say, *"I love chocolate."* I'm told that women are the experts at this kind of love. Now, if love is of God, storge love could well be the kind of love that God has when taking delight in creation. *"And God saw that it was good."* So to love chocolate is a good thing, as is to love nature, beautiful sunsets and newborn babies. Did you ever wonder why so many of us feel close to God at such times? Could it not be that God is touching us in a special way through *storge* love? It's part of love's mystery.

Then, there is *philia* love. Philadelphia is the city of *philia* love; that is "of brotherly love." If a guy says he loves his wife like a sister, she shouldn't be flattered. It is love, but not the kind of love that makes for a great marriage, although this kind of love compliments and certainly enhances marital love. Since *philia* love is also the love of friendship, it is the kind of love children should be encouraged to have with other kids, and especially teenagers who are just beginning to date since it lets them discover and respect the differences between male and female, boys and girls, men and women.

Philia love can be courageous, as has been shown time and time again on the battlefields of history. There is a special dimension of loyalty to it, even an "all-for-one-one-for-all" kind of fidelity. Although the Israelites abandoned God and were unfaithful, God remained faithful to them. Again, could it be that fidelity is a quality of love because we are made in the divine image?

It's important that married couples throw in a little *eros* love. This erotic love is a love of pleasure, often identified with sexual love. I don't watch "reality" television, especially those bachelor/bachelorette type shows, but I think they are pretty much about erotic love. In fact, when our culture speaks of love it seems to have this in mind most of the time. While there is certainly nothing wrong with it in itself, it may not be appropriate with a particular person at this time or in this place, as it leads to sexual intimacy. What is beautiful about it is the longing the two lovers have for each other. The lovely book in the Hebrew scripture, _The Song of Songs_, uses two lovers to represent the longing that God has for his chosen people. Could it be that the longing a soldier has to be home again with his wife and children is just a variation on the theme of this kind of love? I find it interesting that the root meaning of the word diabolic is to separate or to divide. Thus, the work of Satan is to divide, to split, to segregate people, even to isolate us one from another. If that is so, it seems reasonable that the work of bringing people together is divine work, the work of the Spirit. Yes, God is present in _eros_ love, too.

Even though these three kinds of love have much to commend them, none is the kind of love that we have most in mind when we speak of a priest as an _alter Christus_ or of our couples as living sacraments of Christ's love. That kind of love has a special name. It is called _agape_ love. It is a selfless love of others that asks for nothing in return. This kind of love is other-centered, self-giving and self-sacrificing. It gives itself away so its beloved can live. It can be very profound, as when Jesus says, _"No one has greater love than this, to lay down one's life for his friends"_ (John 15:13). But our prime example of _agape_ love is Jesus on the cross. This is the highest form of love. Jesus loved us to the end. Love alone was reason enough for Jesus to offer himself on the cross for us. Anyone who is familiar with Lawrence Kohlberg's work on the stages of moral development will recognize _agape_ love as the motive for decision making at the sixth and highest stage of moral behavior. You do something because it is the loving thing to do.

> A popular story is told of a little girl dying of a disease from which her eight year old brother had recovered some time before. The doctor said to the boy, _"Only a transfusion of your blood will save the life of your sister._

Are you willing to give her your blood?" The eyes of the boy widened in fear. He hesitated for a while, then finally answered, *"Okay, doctor. I'll do it."* An hour after the transfusion was completed the boy asked hesitantly, *"Say, doctor, when do I die?"* It was only then that the doctor understood the momentary fear that had seized the child. He had thought that in giving his blood he was giving his life for his sister.

Philia love had become *agape* love. The little brother was willing to give his life so his sister could live.

A lot of young couples come to the church to get married. The question that always goes through my mind is whether or not they have the kind of love of which marriages are made. There is no question that they love each other. They want each other. But are they ready to surrender their lives to each other so that their spouse can live life to the full? hat is the kind of love of which marriages are made. I'm tempted to ask them both if they are ready to die for each other just to see the look on their faces. Is it even possible for them to have that kind of love when they come to get married? Maybe, maybe not. But the desire for that kind of self-giving love is often there, and that can be enough to start. It will grow with God's grace that comes through experience, with encouragement, in time and by learning the ways of love. At least that's my prayer.

* * * * * * *

How do our young people learn that their love isn't just about them? I think that has to be learned over time also, but it can be taught early on in the way they experience life growing up. The modeling of parents is critical, not to mention good catechesis on the social nature of the gospel of Jesus. We can take advantage of teachable moments that come along, like when teens start dating. For example, it is most natural for parents to ask their daughter or son when they come home from a date, *"Did you have a good time?"* That's okay. They are interested in what is happening to their child after all. But I suggest they ask another question, an even more important question. It will turn their evening out into a learning experience they hadn't thought about. *"Did your date have a good time?"* This is letting them know that a healthy relationship, and eventually genuine love, is not just about oneself. It's about someone else. In a culture that worships the trinity of "me, myself and I," it's a lesson that needs to be taught early on.

While marital love is not just about oneself, it's not just about fulfilling duties and meeting the needs of another, either. It is essentially a gift, a generous offer of oneself to the other. While many desires and needs of a husband are met in his love relationship with his wife, his motive for maintaining their relationship is his love for her. And while he may meet many of her needs, he, above all, wants to enable her by his love to enjoy the fullness of life. This will help shape her sense of worth, belonging, personal identity and sense of freedom she needs to live her life as a married woman.

When Genesis says, *"It is not good for the man to be alone,"* it isn't saying he needs someone to love him as much as he needs to have someone to love, someone who will receive his love. And, ironically, in giving himself so totally to his wife, the husband experiences his own fulfillment as a man. In giving herself away to her husband, the wife experiences her fulfillment as a woman. When scripture says, *"It is in our giving that we receive."* it need not be about money at all. Our modern world says we find fulfillment in getting more and more, while Jesus, in effect, says just the opposite. *"Give yourself away in love, and you will find yourself; surrender yourself to your beloved in love and you will be your best self. At such times you will sense a joy that no one can take from you."*

We're not talking pre-nuptials arrangements here. We're not talking a 50-50 proposition. We are talking covenant, the free giving of self to another in love; a 100% - 100% giving proposition. It's only when a couple begins to falter in their love for each other that they start thinking in terms of fairness and justice and rights. When we speak of agape love, one's focus is primarily on the well being of the other, rather than self. St.

Paul's notable passage on marriage in his letter to the Ephesians tries to underscore this very point when he speaks of the mutual subordination husbands and wives are to have for each other. You know the passage. *"Wives should be submissive to their husbands as to the Lord because the husband is head of his wife just as Christ is head of his body, the church, as its savior. As the church submits to Christ, so wives should submit to their husbands. Husbands, love your wives, as Christ loved the church. He gave himself up for her to make her holy. . . Husbands should love their wives as they do their own bodies"* (Eph. 5: 21-25).

Quite frankly, I hate to hear this passage read in church. The women stop listening when they hear the *"be submissive to your husbands"* part, the very moment when the men start listening. I'm afraid that that's all they hear. They can miss entirely the *"he gave himself up for her"* part. The issue is <u>mutual</u> submission. As husbands and wives, they give themselves to each other. They are servants of each other. Sadly, this beautiful passage has led to a so-called "chain of command" theology that some have used to justify the domination of women, while it actually calls each party to take their eyes off of themselves and any "what's in it for me" attitude they may have. Rather than being an "out of step with the modern world" passage, it underscores the dignity of both men and women and challenges them to live accordingly. St. Paul goes on to say that this is a great mystery with many implications. And why not? The couple's agape love is inexorably intertwined with Christ's love. At such times his joy is within them; they sense it, and their joy is complete.

* * * * * * *

But we don't have to use such dramatic examples as the domination of women or the abuse scandal to see how our sacramental couples call the church to the depth of agape love. I remember Billy Graham saying in one of his crusades, *"I have never been tempted to divorce my wife. Divorce has never crossed my mind; murder maybe, but never divorce!"* This was his humorous way of saying that love, even of spouse, is not always easy. If we are not careful, a couple's relationship can slip into little more than the fulfilling duties to each other. Yet, their commitment to love, not to mention the grace of the Sacrament of Matrimony, beckons that same couple to choose to love anyway, even when they don't feel like it.

Do you think Jesus *felt* loving when he was hanging on the cross? I can't imagine it. If he was looking at us, he was seeing us in our weakness and our sin. It was not a pretty sight. Yet, he chose to love us anyway, to the end. *"Love one another as I have loved you"* beckons our sacramental couples to love each other beyond attraction. And they do it, even in the little, irritating things of life. For example, I wonder what a new husband thinks when he wakes up in the morning and sees his wife drool or something like that?! Just wondering.

Well, anyway, here's the amazing part. When we human beings love, we love because we are attracted to the one we love. We are drawn to beauty and goodness like a moth to flame whether they are physical, psychological or spiritual. But divine love is different. When God loves us, it isn't that God sees our beauty and goodness and then loves us because of what he sees. Rather, when God loves, God bestows beauty and goodness. God loves goodness and beauty into us. God bestows attractiveness upon us.

Because our couples are a Sacrament of Christ's love, when they love, they bestow goodness and beauty on each other. They make each other more attractive. And, I would venture to add, more holy, because holiness is all about living in the spirit of divine love. And this helps bring out the goodness of their beloved, especially at those times when he or she is not feeling very worthy of love.

What a gift that is! When one doesn't feel very loveable, a spouse can love the gift of love into them! And when they love their children, they are also bestowing attractiveness on them, too. In light of this awareness, we can see why a sin like criticism in the family is such a terrible thing. Not only does it cripple a couple's love for each other, it negates the effect of their love on each other and on their children.

At times when I've been around certain couples, I've caught myself silently saying things like, *"I wonder what she sees in him?"* or *"Boy am I glad I'm not married to her."* He might be a blowhard and she might be a blabbermouth. But what I think really doesn't matter. What matters is that they love each other. And when we look at people with the eyes of love, we are bound to see goodness and beauty, and even bestow it. I recall the time I was giving a Marriage Encounter weekend with a couple who would hardly be confused with Ken and Barbie. Yet, when the husband described his wife sitting right next to him, you'd think he was describing Julia Roberts from the movie "Pretty Woman." I recall glancing over toward them in wondering admiration.

* * * * * * *

The implications of loving beyond attraction should be clear regarding how we are to love in the church. We are not just expected to love one another when it is easy. Sometimes we are expected to love one another when it is hard, when we are unattractive. As a pastor, I certainly wasn't attracted to everyone in my parish. At times, I'd find myself trying to avoid certain people. Some people are not all that beautiful. Oh, they may be pleasant to look at, but instead of having joyful hearts, they are complainers, blamers, fault finders, and all around negative people. You know the type. Who wants to be around them? (I pray for their spouses.)

> Reminds me of the time Satan appeared during a church service. He let out a mighty roar, and scared off everyone on his right. He roared again, and scared off everyone on his left. Then he noticed one guy who hadn't budged. He just stood there. So Satan goes up to him and roars right in his face. The guy doesn't flinch. Satan roars again; again, no response from the guy. So Satan says to him with as intimidating a voice as he can muster, *"I am the devil and you are supposed to be afraid of me!"* *"Why?"* asked the man. *"I've been married to your sister for 27 years."*

Some people are not very attractive, but does that make them less deserving of my love? Of course not! I still have to love them. I have yet to find a passage in the gospel that dispenses me. And it's all our sacramental couples' fault! They won't let me forget. Why? Because they continue to love each other even when they don't feel like it, as when one's spouse complains, blames, gets angry or finds fault. It must take a special grace of some kind. Here's the point. They remind me of the way Jesus loves us. What St. Paul said must be true. *"Love bears all things."*

Our couples model for us a love beyond attraction. They model love the way Jesus loves. Actually, they do more than that. They don't just model his love. As living sacraments, I believe they actually make Jesus' love tangible, real, right here, right now. Rather than just model agape love for me, I believe they even enable, empower me to love unattractive people. Aren't they sacraments of Christ's love? Don't sacraments bestow what they signify? What would happen if it dawned on our couples what extraordinary power they have to touch the lives of others? They would certainly have greater respect for themselves as Sacraments of the Church, and be truly humbled by that awareness. So would we. It's just another surprise!

CONVERSATION STARTERS:

1. What is the main thing in your marriage?

2. How does your vocation to make Christ's love real in your world strike you?

3. How might Christ's love show itself through your relationship?

4. I what ways do you see your spouse "die" for you?

5. How might you bestow goodness on each other or your children?

CHAPTER SEVEN

BEARERS OF HOPE

"But you know how I step on toes."

A priest and a nun were on a mission together in the backwoods of Appalachia. As the sun was setting, they realized they were hopelessly lost and that they wouldn't find their way home that night. Deep in the nearby woods they saw a cabin, so they went to check it out. Fortunately, it was unlocked so they could spend the night there. Unfortunately, it had only one bed. But they found some blankets and an old sleeping bag, so they knew they'd be okay. The nun got the bed and the priest slept on the floor in the sleeping bag. After a few minutes, the nun started to complain about the cold. Shivering, she asked the priest, *"Would you mind getting me another blanket?"* So the priest got up and got her another blanket. As he was about to fall asleep a bit later, she said through chattering teeth, *"Oh, Father, would you get me another blanket?"* So he got up again and got her yet another blanket. A third time, she complained about the cold, so he said, *"Sister, I think I have the solution. For tonight only, what do you think about our acting like a husband and wife?"* Staring into the dark she said, *"To stay warm, I suppose that would be okay."* *"Good!"* the priest said. *"Get up and get your own blanket!"*

* * * * * * *

Honeymoons don't last forever, no matter how wonderful they were. And nobody lives happily ever after, either. In fact, I am always leery of couples who say that they never fight. In such cases, my suspicion is that one party is probably controlling the other, while the other is stuffing all kinds of negative emotions. Any dominant-submissive relationship cannot be all that healthy; and there is certainly no family resemblance to the relationship of love in the Trinity, for in the Trinity there is a total equality of persons. Too many couples have learned that peace at any price is very expensive. What they experience is not really peace anyway; at least not in the biblical sense of shalom peace. Peace is so much more than freedom from conflict. It must include the freedom to live life to the full.

But even when there is peace in a home, and the couple has a healthy relationship, and their loving dance together is filled with joy, they still can't help but step on each other's toes now and then. After all, some of the dance steps in the ways of love can be difficult to learn. But if our goal is to learn how to love, take heart. We can often learn more from our mistakes than we can from doing everything right, and God knows we are on this earth to learn.

In other words, we need to accept the obvious fact that we are not perfect at love. No one is. And as much as a couple might want to go back to the joy of their honeymoon, they can't. They know too much about each other, especially the weaknesses and flaws that poked their heads up during their time of daily living so closely together. This reminds me of the man who was looking for the perfect woman to be his wife. She had to be well educated, serious but fun, a person of deep faith, etc. Finally, he found a woman who met all of his requirements so he asked her to marry him. *"Sorry,"* she said. *"I'm looking for the perfect man."*

Even when a couple thinks they made every effort to do everything right, things happen that can cause them to wonder. How many parents tend to blame themselves because a son or daughter leaves the church, marries outside the church, or has a child out of wedlock? *"Where did we go wrong?"* they ask. Notice, they tend to blame themselves first since they hold their beloved child in such esteem. It may or may not have been their fault at all, but they can't help themselves. Fr. Ron Rolheiser, O.M.I. said something in his book **"The Holy Longing"** [1] that I think could give consolation to those parents, especially if they fear for their children who have drifted away from Christ, whom they so wanted for them to have in their lives. Rolheiser reminds them that when their "wayward" son or daughter touches them, they touch the Body of Christ. But there is even more. Since the couple is a sacrament of Christ's love, when they show love for their child, Jesus is loving them as well. Jesus is not far from them at all, certainly not as far as many parents may fear.

This is why it is important for parents to maintain as close a relationship as possible with those children, especially when they have let them down in some way. This is why issuing a threat like, *"If you get pregnant, you will no longer be a daughter of mine; you can pack your bags and get out!"* is more counterproductive than anything. What good does it do? Such a statement says more about the parent than the child. Granted, the mother and father may be crushed, but we don't overcome evil with more evil. The question they need to ask in this situation is, *"What does our love for our daughter look like in this situation?"* Kicking her out sure doesn't look very loving to me.

Should a daughter think that her father will actually kick her out of the house should she become pregnant, she will not only feel the rejection keenly, she will also be more apt to look for a way to avoid that humiliation and punishment. And one of the most obvious ways out of the anticipated rejection would be to seek an abortion. After all, her father would never find out and the immediate crisis would be over. Regrettably, this has no doubt happened too many times to our Catholic girls.

Sadly, it is not difficult to see a parallel to this very behavior in the church. I can't help but wonder about the wisdom of any policy that automatically removes a person from ministry who violates some moral standard when doing so can be easily interpreted as violating our call as Christians to be merciful. I have in mind both professionals ministers and volunteers. While dismissal may eventually be the final decision, it should not be a "one strike and you're out" situation. "One size fits all" doesn't fit. There is a huge difference between a one time act (getting pregnant) and a choice that becomes one's lifestyle (living together with one's boy/girlfriend). In the first case, sorrow and repentance are most often part of the story, but not in the on-going choice to defy church teaching. Circumstances are seldom the same.

Furthermore, like in a family, good can come from a bad situation if it is used as a teachable moment. Without compromising for a moment the church's teaching on premarital sex, a strong, shepherd leader could help everyone see that harsh discipline could actually do more harm than good, as in the pushing of the young woman toward the tragedy of abortion, thus sending the message that she was no longer valued by the faith community or welcome in it because of her sin (biblical echoes of being unclean), and that from now on she would be on her own. Is that the message we want the church to send?

Instead, what if the pro's and con's were carefully weighed, considering such things as the young woman's need for support and a community of faith to belong to before and after the baby's birth? While there is admittedly an element of scandal present, it need not evolve into the far greater scandal of moral rigidity born of a narrow-minded self-righteousness. While proclaiming the values of right and wrong, we don't have to compromise them or the values of compassion and forgiveness. I've known many wonderful people during my fifty years as a priest who, despite a time of moral lapse, have straightened their lives out and went on to serve the church well and without scandal. We do believe in redemption, don't we? We can't let rules make our decisions for us. They are too easy to hide behind, and make it too easy to blame the rule maker rather than accept responsibility for the decision ourselves. At their best, they serve as statements of our values and should help guide us to make the best decisions we can under the circumstances.

However, even if the institutional church turns its back on a young woman who gets pregnant, it is important to remember that her parents are still a sacrament of Jesus' love for her. Jesus does not just touch her through mom and dad; Jesus loves her through mom and dad. He never stopped loving the people in his life, not even Judas or Pilate. For this reason, it always hurts to hear that the church, which is called to love as Jesus loves, fails to do so. The difficult truth is that we are never dispensed from loving no matter what happens. As living sacraments of Christ's love, this is easy to understand with parents. It should be just as easy to understand with the church. After all, if the depth of love is not mercy, what is it? What's the point of identifying the Second Sunday of Easter "Mercy Sunday" if we just wink at mercy the rest of the year?

In our couples, their love is entwined with Christ's; not just in good times but in bad times as well. The love that helped create their children and that surrounded them when growing up can still have a place to play in helping them return home or back to their faith if that's the issue. Children are very often as close to Christ as they are to their parents. I think the difference between the parents and the church is that parents know better than to expect perfection from their children. I don't think Jesus expects it from us, either.

But what about that statement in the gospel of Matthew when Jesus says we are *"to be perfect like your heavenly Father is perfect"* (Matt. 5:48)? Unfortunately, a lot of people have beaten themselves up over this verse, thinking it expresses the Greek idea of moral perfection that they should strive to live up to but can't because it is impossible. However, Jesus didn't live out of a Greek mindset. What he is saying is in effect, *"If God's love is boundless, so should yours be boundless."* Actually, they are like the words of Jesus in the new commandment: *"Love one another as I have loved you."* We'll never live up to them, either. But they do something very important for us. They give direction to our lives. They are very close to saying the same thing, as Jesus always did the will of his Father. The context of this passage makes it clear that the perfection that Jesus asks of us is in loving the way the Father loves us, even our enemies. We are being called, even expected, to love imperfect people, including ourselves. In short, love no matter what. That is what we must strive to be perfect at, not only in the family but also in the church. Only when love is somehow a part of our response to evil will we be overcoming evil with good. After all, attempting to overcome evil with evil just makes for more evil.

Of course, now and again we bump into some people who apparently believe they are living the moral perfection that they mistakenly think Jesus called for. Sadly, they are often very judgmental of others who simply don't measure up. St. Teresa of Avila has an observation worth thinking about. Speaking of someone she had met she said, *"She and two other souls that I have seen..., who were saints in their own opinion, caused me more fear, after I spoke with them, than all the sinners I have seen."* [2] It's like someone who is proud of their purity. What's the point?

* * * * * * *

The surprising truth is that our sacramental couples have much to teach us precisely because they are flawed! Granted, our couples inflict pain on each other even though they love each other. It happens. Sometimes it's in small things, but it can also be in big things. And it is at these difficult times, when they decide to love in spite of a hurt, that their love can be most Christ-like and efficacious . . . and most difficult. They express that kind of love that is absolutely necessary for any love relationship to survive, not to mention grow. It is the kind of love that Jesus showed time and time again: a forgiving, reconciling love. For like Jesus, couples don't just love because it feels good. Times come when they have to choose to love even if it hurts.

Love is not just a feeling we act upon. Often, love is a decision we have to make to do something that is hard, with all kinds of negative feelings attached. But a properly motivated couple will choose to love because on their wedding day they committed to love each other *"in good times and in bad,"* and they meant it! They choose to love in order to restore the flow of love between them, for without forgiveness, the "air" between them may not just be stagnant, it may even be foul. And foul air can suffocate. It is as if their relationship has stopped breathing. And unless they can get it started again, their relationship will die. In short, without forgiveness, they will have no future.

The fact that a couple is a sacrament of the church doesn't mean they always live up to it. For example, a woman told me of the struggle she had forgiving her husband who had been unfaithful. Her faith told her she had to forgive him, but she just couldn't bring herself to do so. She knew what to do but she just didn't want to do it, even though her husband had repeatedly said he was sorry. He had done all he could. The ball was now in her court. The weight of their sad story had now shifted to her shoulders.

"But what if he doesn't mean it?" she said fearfully. I think this is the crux of the problem: the fear to trust that it will work out. How do we trust someone again who has been unfaithful to us? This is a legitimate concern. To trust again means to leave oneself open to be hurt again, and who wants to do that? It is certainly a risk. However, if we turn to the gospel for guidance, we see that the one thing Jesus never showed was harshness toward known sinners and/or the weak. He attends to them with gentleness and concern. After all, he loves them, and without that love, trust is virtually impossible.

If the call to forgive has found a place in our hearts, it will prevent us from doing more damage. Quoting Isaiah, Jesus describes the suffering servant of God in these words: *"He will not break a bruised reed or snuff out a smoldering wick"* (Matt: 12:20). Such was the condition of his heart, a sign of the kingdom he preached. There is no mention of getting even, punishing or dismissing the sinner from his life. Apparently, Jesus sees value in the weak person, the sinner that others simply do not, cannot or will not see.

Certainly, to be trusted again, the one who has broken faith must have a change of heart, true repentance, a desire to make things right. Granted, there may also come a time when it becomes clear that certain people are simply not trustworthy, and in such cases it may be best to move on. But trust does not require absolute certitude that something will never happen again. If it did, we wouldn't forgive anyone, and Jesus' statement to Peter about forgiving sinners 70 x 7 times wouldn't make any sense. And the consequences of not forgiving would do far more harm than good.

To be quite frank, I don't think we can come to this kind of love without looking to Jesus and drawing strength from him. This could well be the frequent focus of a married person's daily reflection on the gospel.

It is full of stories that reveal a characteristic about Jesus that we may never have noticed before, such as the times when he healed the woman with the hemorrhage, raised the official's daughter to life, cured the two blind men who appealed to him for mercy, or the woman caught in the act of adultery. Clearly, they tell us Jesus is a compassionate wonderworker, but we know that. If we read the stories carefully, though, we notice that Jesus never says he healed anyone. He says things like, *"Your faith has saved you."* Jesus sees something in the people in need that contributes to their healing. In spite of their sin and/or weakness, he sees goodness. Often, when we are hurt, all we can see is just the hurt, and it blinds us to any goodness upon which to build a base for reconciliation.

But there is even more. We discover that, when Jesus encounters people who are hurting, he can't seem to help himself. He was drawn to them, like there is something about him that cannot resist reaching out to heal, to comfort, to calm and to forgive. It's as if he was compelled to eat with outcasts and sinners. And when we remember that he is divine love incarnate, we get an insight into what divine love looks like in the here and now situations of life. The problem is that we are so familiar with the gospel stories of Jesus that it's unthinkable that he wouldn't be compassionate even though we struggle with it ourselves. Let's make it as clear as possible. Compassion for the wounded, suffering and alienated is a divine quality, a quality so important that if it were not there, the gospels themselves would be gutted of meaning. There would be no hope for any of us!

* * * * * * *

Some might say that there is a soft spot in Jesus' heart for us, for our hurting humanity. Or to put this in an even more shocking way, we can say that the God of biblical revelation suffers. While we say with philosophers that God is *"all powerful, all wise and all knowing,"* implying *"without weakness,"* in the Jesus of the gospel we see pain. I don't just mean the physical pain that Jesus would feel as a man who might cut his finger with a knife. I mean that deep inner pain that comes from sensing hurt or loss, even the hurt and loss experienced in others. Jesus wept at the death of Lazarus. It is a pain that is born of love. Without Jesus' extraordinary love for us, he would not have wept over Jerusalem in frustration, *"like a mother hen who just wanted to gather her chicks under her wings, but they wouldn't let me" (Matt. 23:37).* Nor would there have been any agony in the Garden of Gethsemane. A garden in the scriptures is always a place of love. Gethsemane is that garden where Jesus sweats blood in the agony of loneliness because no one will receive his love. Love is what Jesus does because love is who Jesus is. He can't help himself.

Since Jesus has this "soft spot" for the hurting, some may conclude that he plays favorites. I don't think so. Jesus loves all the people on earth with an unconditional love. No one is excluded from his love, as his love embraces everyone. But when one of us is hurting that is the one who gets his special attention. After all, what parent would not do the same for a hurting child? They love all their kids, but it is the sick one that gets their attention. They can't help themselves. They have to do whatever they can to comfort and heal. Part of the challenge of having a sick child is not ignoring their other children.

When couples act like this, out of compassion for the hurting and suffering, I truly believe that it is evidence of the power of God at work in their lives, that their love is truly blended in with God's love. They don't have to be told what to do. In some way they even enter into divine suffering, that is, when they suffer because they love, it may just be that they are experiencing a bit of the suffering of God. While this compassionate love is not limited to our married couples, they serve to remind the church that we are all called to be compassionate for the weak and hurting.

Suffering, in other words, may be a way God reveals the depth of divine love for us. It may even be a tangible hint at the measure of it. Therefore, since we are made in the image of God, our showing compassion should be a given just as it is in Jesus. Clearly, those who ignore or take advantage of the weak and hurting are not acting out of the Spirit of God, nor are they living their own dignity as human beings. But before we start throwing stones at someone else, we know we have all done the same because we are all broken, wounded and imperfect at love.

Didn't Jesus say, *"Blessed are they who mourn?"* Well, I can't will myself to mourn. Such a feeling is a spontaneous response that comes from someplace deep inside of me. What I am suggesting is that we mourn because we are in touch with the Spirit of God dwelling in our hearts. We can't help ourselves. When we have that capacity, we are blessed. If we don't mourn when we see suffering, even of distant people in war torn places like Iraq or Afghanistan, it may well mean that we are not in touch with the Spirit dwelling in our hearts. We are not living up to our dignity as human beings. Call it the "preferential option for the poor" or whatever, but it shows that God wants to touch our world through us.

When Jesus saw peoples' wounds, he responded with his healing love. He healed the sick, clothed the naked, gave sight to the blind and forgave the sinner. I believe this compassionate quality of divine love is meant for all of us. That's what the judgment scene in Matthew 25 is all about when Jesus separates the sheep from the goats. When we act on that inner Spirit of compassion, we may not even be aware of it. I simply do not see how we can learn the ways of love without learning the ways of Jesus. And we cannot learn the ways of Jesus without learning the ways of suffering love. It seems to me, then, that if we take learning how to love seriously, forgiveness seriously, we will take our faith seriously! Taking this one step further, we will take the cross seriously.

* * * * * * *

Now, what has all this got to do with couples who hurt each other, especially when healing or forgiveness is called for? Well, after initial anger, which hinders and possibly stops the flow of love between them and may cause a form of temporary moral blindness, couples will eventually want to reestablish the movement of love between their hearts. Sooner or later they will see the other's hurt, not just their own, and then be drawn to reach out to the other to heal and forgive. When they realize what they have done to the person they are committed to love, they will also feel pain, and that pain urges them to reach out and seek reconciliation. Just as Jesus couldn't ignore the wounds of the hurting, neither can they, especially those wounds they may have caused.

I recall a documentary on television of a young girl about seven years of age who had a rare neurological disorder called Congenital Insensitivity to Pain with Anhidrosis (CIPA). She could not feel pain. Something was wrong with her nervous system. If she were to put her hand on a hot stove, she wouldn't feel it because it wouldn't send the pain signal to her brain. She once jumped off a table and broke her leg and then walked on it like nothing had happened, thus doing further damage. She could not live a normal life. So we need to be careful when we say we want a world free of pain.

For all the agony that pain causes, some pain can be a good thing. Pain is important. It is often telling us that something needs attention, healing, correction or forgiveness. Pain is like the warning light on the dashboard of a car. When it goes on, we'd better find out what's wrong or we could do serious damage to our car. Remember what C.S. Lewis said about the dangers of wanting to be free of the pain that comes from love. Heaven alone is that reality that has love without pain, and this isn't heaven.

Secular society's efforts to deaden the human conscience and to eliminate the pain of guilt from the human heart have had tragic consequences. The prevalence of abortion is an obvious example. It is not politically correct to speak of the morality of such an act. That might make someone feel guilty! Rather than being considered either moral or immoral, it is simply amoral. Its rightness or wrongness is a non-issue. It doesn't matter. We are told such actions have no morality attached to them at all; they are neither right nor wrong. Consequently, the pain caused by guilt becomes something silly and old fashioned and thus never has to be dealt with. We might as well be running around on a broken leg because we are doing severe damage to ourselves, to others, and even to the moral fiber of our nation, not to mention the obvious victim, the unborn child.

Our rationalizations sidestep the sin and try to justify the behavior even though our guts tell us something is wrong. So we say things like,

"But it's legal." or *"Everybody's doing it."* And if that doesn't work, we play our ace: *"What does the Catholic Church know about it anyway?"* or *"Who does it think it is to tell us what to do?"* The fact that some leave the church over moral issues is very predictable because they really can't say they believe one thing and then do the contrary for any length of time. Sooner or later something has to give. Besides, there is a vocal part of our secular culture that will not support anything the church teaches, particularly of a sexual nature. This is a negative application of Wayne Dyer's observation, *"When we change the way we look at things, the things we look at change."* No wonder religion is ridiculed by the "amoral" trendsetters of our secular society.

By the way, I am not trying to reinstate the notion of "Catholic guilt" here. But a dose of real guilt now and then can be very healthy. When I was a growing up, a priest told me that the human conscience was like a three cornered wheel in my chest. When I did something wrong, it would begin to spin, and it would hurt as the corners dug into my heart. But the longer I continued to do it, the corners gradually wore down until it was round and smooth. It still spun when I did something wrong, but I no longer felt it. While today I can hardly remember what I had for breakfast, I can still remember the priest telling me that, and it was well over 60 years ago. To live a life free of pain can be dangerous to one's health. Life has moral consequences whether we like it or not.

A golfer was sitting in the clubhouse after playing a round. He looked upset. So his friend went over to him asked what was wrong. The golfer said, *"It was terrible. On the 16th hole I sliced one out onto the freeway and it went through the windshield of a bus, and there was a terrible accident. The bus went out of control and hit a car head-on. The dead and injured were all over the place."* The friend said, *"That's awful. What did you do?"* *"Well, I closed up my stance and shortened my backswing a little."*

We excuse ourselves and then try to forget what we have done. For countless people, of course, it doesn't work, and they live with a hole in their hearts that they can't fill. Some try to escape the emptiness by climbing the ladder of success, or perhaps by exotic travel, or by hyper-activity; some take pain-killers in the form of mindless TV watching, endless internet surfing, or by drifting gradually into the deadening worlds of drugs, sex and alcohol. But they don't work. In time, the weight of it all pulls them down. I've seen it in women who have suffered through the tragedy of an abortion they had experienced years earlier. Feelings of guilt eventually surface. Remorse says there is a wound somewhere deep inside that needs attention; that needs healing. But even simple things like anxiety in a relationship says something may be haywire, and we'd better find out what that something is lest it fester and cause real damage. Only when we find out what it is can we then do anything about it.

* * * * * * *

So often the last thing we want to admit about ourselves is that we are wounded and need help. Our egos resist facing the truth of our weakness, but the fact remains, our sins wound us. Often, the guilty party doesn't know how to express their feelings except by saying, *"I don't know what's wrong, but something is missing in my life."* And what is missing is not religion. Many come back to the Catholic Church and nothing happens, except to feel more guilt. Some try other churches, but that doesn't work either.

What is missing is the flow of grace in their hearts, or, as we've been saying, the flow of divine love. Their relationship with the God who is love has been broken. Their sin has blocked the flow of the Spirit in their lives. That's what sin does. That's why they feel empty. The very thing they were created for - to share in the flow of the divine life of the Trinity - is not there! They discover that denial doesn't work, nor do all those things they use to deaden the pain. Pretending it isn't there is, after all, pretending. Even attempts at self affirmation come up empty. There comes a point when they realize that they have to face their sin head on, admit it, and then do what they need to do to heal it. It is time to face the truth.

We're not too different from the alcoholic who cannot admit he has a drinking problem, when, in fact, it could be ruining his life, his family, his future, and all because he can't see that drinking has taken control of him. The only way God can break into his heart is to go directly through his wound. This means that he must admit he has a wound in the first place, and that he is powerless to do anything about it by himself. And that is the first step of the twelve steps of Alcoholics Anonymous.

The only people Jesus ever really got angry with were those who wore the cloak of righteousness and would not admit their sin, those whom he sadly called *"whited sepulchers."* As he said, *"I came for the sick, not the healthy"* (Matt. 9:12). Sin blocks the work of the Holy Spirit in our lives, and that blockage sends a pain through us that demands our attention as much as the pain that runs down our arm before a heart attack. And that means we are wounded, so wounded, perhaps, that it inhibits our ability to make God's love present and real in our world, which is our vocation as followers of Jesus in the first place.

Admitting our wound is what opens our hearts to the soothing grace of Jesus. What a blessing to have the Sacrament of Reconciliation (Confession). I don't know of any other time or place when a priest is more challenged to show a depth of love for a broken person than during the celebration of this extraordinary sacrament of healing. It can be the end of suffering caused by something that happened years before, and the beginning of relief. The reason we begin Mass by seeking God's mercy in the Penitential Rite is because that will help open our hearts to the power of God's Word and the healing grace of the Eucharist.

Because we live in a world that won't admit of weakness or show vulnerability of any kind, our egos will resist and fight any admission that we need forgiveness from anyone, even the church through confession. I believe it was Richard Rohr who said, *"To receive God's forgiving grace is a humiliation to our ego."* Our ego defies any implication that it is not in control. While we wear the façade of righteousness, we, in truth, cause hurt to the very ones we are committed to love. And we are often mystified why. We need to admit we are weak and in need of God's merciful grace. And once we admit our wound, we open a way for God to enter our hearts and restore the flow of his saving love. We have God's attention, not because we are so good and attractive, but because we are wounded and in need of divine healing.

* * * * * *

Our sins, rather than disqualify us from God's love, in fact, make us prime candidates for God's mercy. But, like the people in the gospel stories, we have to bring something to the table. There is something in us that is crucial to the healing process. We must admit we are wounded, that we have sinned, that we are sorry, and then turn in faith to Jesus believing he will forgive us. Like when we go to our doctor, Jesus asks us, *"Where do you hurt?" "What do you want me to do for you?"* And when we say what it is, we know the Jesus will heal our spirit, thus setting us free to live life to the full again by inviting us back into the life-giving flow of divine love.

Again, in the spirit of A.A., telling another human being one's story somehow helps the healing process. There is much wisdom in taking advantage of the Sacrament of Reconciliation. That's why it is so important to us Catholics. After receiving the mercy of God through the church, we will not be tempted to feel defensive when we say *"Lord, I am not worthy..."* before receiving Holy Communion at Mass. We will know we are not worthy, but our humbled ego will know also that that isn't the issue anymore. The issue is God's love for us in spite of our unworthiness. God pours his healing love into us and thus invites us to the Eucharistic banquet. Because of mercy, we realize that it's not about us at all, but the wonder of God's overwhelming love. And gathered with us is a whole church full of broken and wounded people; all candidates for mercy. Like so long ago, Jesus still can't help himself, for, even in our own day, he welcomes sinners and eats with them, lay and clergy alike.

The bishop called an older pastor into his office. *"Father,"* the bishop said, *"I hear that in that part of the Eucharistic Prayer when you mention my name, you also add the words, 'your unworthy servant.' You shouldn't be doing that."* In response, the old priest said, *"But isn't that what you say?"* *"Yes it is,"* said the bishop, *"but you make it sound like you mean it."*

Maybe we all need to remind ourselves that we are wounded. It keeps us humble, and that is good for the ego. This could be why an alcoholic introduces himself by saying, *"Hello, my name is Boyd, and I am an alcoholic."* I've found that in my life I spend a lot more time fighting God than fighting Satan, and it is a battle I hope to lose.

The Gospel of Jesus is an on-going call to love. In the replaced Eucharistic Prayer #2 we prayed, *"Lord, remember your Church throughout the world; <u>make us grow in love,</u> together with Benedict, our pope, Raymond, our bishop, and all the clergy...."* This is not just a nice idea, but the vision of the Church herself. It is an invitation to an ever-continuing conversion of heart. It is a call to keep growing in our loving relationships with God and the people in our lives. And when something threatens those relationships, the way we respond is critical. It can either make or break a faith community as easily as it can make or break a marriage.

* * * * * * *

As we said in the last chapter, regardless of what issue couples may fight over, like money, career, in-laws, sex or children, the issue isn't really money, careers, in-laws, sex or children. The critical issue is how these issues affect their relationship with each other (the main thing). Also, should there be something pathological about their relationship, and when it defies the prospect of healing, it is certainly <u>not</u> more important than the health of a spouse or the wellbeing of innocent children. When abusive relationships cannot be healed, those who are in danger have to get out of them! Such relationships are hardly sacramental anyway, certainly not in the sense of anything life-giving that images God's love. The church recognizes this and is ready to help couples deal with the fallout of such tragedies. We may encourage a separation or even divorce in certain situations. And we will do what we can to help those involved continue to live their faith without restriction. We have to.

But here we are talking about those relationships that have been weakened, possibly even shattered by some indiscretion, infidelity, or addiction like to alcohol, to drugs, to gambling or to the "new kid on the block" and equally destructive addiction, pornography on the internet. We are talking about relationships that are still salvageable because both husband and wife still love each other and want to have a future together.

Unlike in simple friendships, just pardoning the offending party is not enough for a married couple. Amnesty is not sufficient. And peaceful co-existence doesn't cut it either. Reconciliation born of true love alone is enough. Hurts must be healed, breaches must be bridged, and emptiness must be filled if a couple is ever to live life to the full again. I believe the graces of the Sacrament of Matrimony offer our couples that kind of help (sacramental grace) which enables them to heal each other so they can be about their sacred vocation in the church. After all, since they are called to be living signs of Christ's love, Jesus will certainly, gracefully, nudge them toward the kind of healing their relationship requires.

A word needs to be said about addictions. Just as there is no way a relationship can be healed as long as a third party is involved, there is no way a relationship can be healed as long as the addiction that is destroying a couple's relationship continues. It is like a "third party" to the relationship. Alcohol takes on the role of a mistress, as do drugs, gambling and pornography. Sadly, an alcoholic, for instance, cannot imagine life without knowing where his next drink is coming from. He can't imagine life without alcohol. But if he wants to keep his marriage, he'd better start! He needs professional help, as do addicted gamblers, drug addicts and those hooked on pornography. They have become slaves to something that is ruining their lives, their marriages and their families. To go to marriage counseling without addressing the addiction is a waste of money and time.

Grace builds on nature, but when one's humanity is so compromised by addiction, there is very little for grace to build upon, or better, there is no way it can freely flow between a couple. Attaining quality sobriety, getting clean, back on the wagon, or whatever you want to call it, must happen before reconciliation is possible in a marriage.

When an estranged couple comes to see me, I am prejudiced in favor of their staying together and working out their problems, especially if they have children. I let them know I believe in them as a sacrament of the church hoping it will empower them to keep trying. I do my best not to pick sides. And knowing my own personal limits, I don't hesitate to send them to professional counseling when it is called for. What is best for them as a sacrament in, of and for the church is my motivation. It may not always work out as I hope, but I have tried to respect them and their calling from God.

Forgiveness and reconciliation are not the same. Fr. Ron Rolheiser, O.M.I. tells the story of the family where one member was so offended by something that he stomped out of the house, slamming the door behind him. He didn't come back for supper, and no one seemed to mind. However, the next morning he decided to come to breakfast, but he didn't say a word to the others who were sitting around the table. Did he want forgiveness? Yes. Do you think they had forgiven him? Yes. Were they reconciled? Not yet. That would take more work.

Our couples need reconciliation, not just forgiveness. Forgiveness restores the flow of love between the two again because the barriers that inhibited the flow of love are at last gone. Reconciliation happens when they express that restored flow of love somehow. Without reconciliation, a couple can't really be a couple, can they? They have to be able to embrace each other in their brokenness to be a couple again. As we said before, no man has the perfect wife. And no wife has the perfect husband. But they both have something even better. They have someone who loves them! And if they don't love each other the way they are, they really don't love each other at all.

A husband can't love his wife the way she used to be, nor can a wife love her husband the way she wants him to become. They must love each other the way they are here and now because that is the only spouse they have. They can't love a memory or a dream. But the good news is they are committed to love each other... and they still have each other. The best news is that forgiveness leads to that moment when they can embrace each other in their brokenness. That is when reconciliation happens. That is when they experience the full flow of love once again that fills the space between them.

Some of the couples that I most admire are the ones who have struggled with their relationships; struggles that I wouldn't wish on my enemies. They know that love is not just a feeling, but above all a decision. While love has feelings attached, it cannot be identified with the various feelings that come and go without warning. So, rather than be manipulated by their feelings, they chose to love... anyway. They chose to remain open... anyway. They chose to forgive... anyway. They chose to embrace... anyway. It is hard to find any other human relationship which is more creative, hopeful and capable of healing the pains of isolation and alienation. This discovery has much to teach us!

* * * * * *

Needless to say, there is need for healing, forgiveness and reconciliation in the church. What I am suggesting here is that we look to our sacramental couples to guide us to this end. They give us hope. Of course, we don't limit our search for solutions to our problems by going to our married couples all the time, but they have something very important to show us. Better than anyone else I know, they show us how to love when it is hard to do so. There are people in the church who are unattractive to us, and we can be tempted to right them off, but our couples living in the spirit of the gospel will tell us, *"Not so fast."* They make it clear that in the church we, like they, must love beyond attraction as well, not only when it is hard to do so, but especially when it is hard to do so.

Think for a second. Are we more apt to hear people say of us Catholics today, *"See how they love one another."* or *"Why all the bickering?"* If you see and hear what I see and hear, we as a church could be doing a whole lot better, and this is true at the parish level, the diocesan level, the national level and possibly even at the universal level. As long as the relationships between priests, bishops and people are in conflict, we cannot just pass it off by saying that it is just the way things are. Our credibility as a church is at stake.

Certainly, the Second Vatican Council gave rise to some of the conflicts, especially between those who accepted the changes it brought and those who resisted them. Some people want to turn things back to the way they were, while others want to press forward. And this tension was and is still keenly felt by priests trying to negotiate the changes of Vatican II. But some of the conflict in the church continues to come as the fall out from the sexual abuse scandal. It is like that story of Br'er Rabbit and the tar baby. We just can't seem to shake ourselves free from it. Then, of course, there are the ordinary frictions and tensions that are present in all communities that come from our fallen human condition.

Let me put it this way. Unlike a married person, as a celibate priest, I don't have someone I can count on in the church who is committed to tell me I am loved anyway, especially if I do something stupid. While Jesus says it sacramentally in Reconciliation and the Eucharist, outside the sacraments, family members and a few friends, I simply can't imagine the institutional church embracing me in my brokenness. On the contrary, I would be seen as an embarrassment, or possibly even worse. I can't imagine what some priests who have been removed from ministry are going through as men, as human beings. When things go wrong, a priest has no one to watch his back.

While I am proud of the church's efforts to reach out to the victims of abuse and their families, and for its efforts to protect the vulnerable by creating and preserving a safe environment in the church for them, we hear very little about the abuser himself after the dust has settled and the final gavel has fallen in a court of law. What happens to him? Is it really okay just to cut him off, and to treat him like he doesn't exist? While our natural instincts may want to do just that because he has caused such hurt, the gospel counsels us to think twice before we do. We can't forget the parable of the weeds and the wheat where Jesus warns us about being too eager to pull out the weeds the enemy has sown, lest good wheat is pulled out with it (Matt. 13:24-30). It may do more harm than good.

Of course, we cannot have people who are a danger to others running free in the church or community. I am in no way advocating that. Some pedophiles end up in prison and rightly so, while others are sent to special facilities designed for them so they can't hurt anyone else. But there are others who just leave, either by their own choice or because they have been laicized. God alone knows where they go or what they do after that. Some religious orders have made efforts to keep such men connected somehow to their communities. Maybe I've missed it, but I just haven't seen this same effort made with diocesan priests. Only time will tell the wisdom of this "out of sight out of mind" practice.

When I read the gospel, I can't find any passage that dispenses us from loving anyone. Therefore, the challenging question that always needs to be asked applies to child abusers as much as to anyone else, the same question parents must ask when a member of their family is in serious trouble: What does love look like in this situation? I don't know the answer, but does it need to look as though we are just washing our hands of them?

Aware of the damage they caused, some may ask, of course, *"Are they worthy of love?"* That's the wrong question just as *"Why do bad things happen to good people?"* is the wrong question. Both imply that love is earned. But love cannot be earned. Love is always a gift. None of us ever earns it . . . from anyone. Our couples know this, and so should everyone else. True, some people are easier to love than others, but love is still to be offered to all somehow. In families, it's done all the time. This may be one reason some prefer not to call the church a family. But it either is or it isn't. We can't have it both ways. We cannot treat it as a family only when it is convenient to do so. At times, it is an inconvenient truth we need to remember. Loving some people can be the most difficult thing we'll ever do. It takes courage.

* * * * * * *

What was the most surprising thing about the story of the gunman, Charles Carl Roberts, who, on October 2, 2006, stormed a one room Amish school house in Lancaster County, Pennsylvania and killed four children, their teacher and wounded five others? It isn't the brutality of the crime, or that he killed them execution style, or that he then turned the gun on himself. It was the response of the Amish community. It forgave him. A victim's grandfather said, *"We must not think evil of this man."* A father said of his child's killer, *"He had a mother, a wife and a soul and now he is standing before a just God."* Amish community members visited and comforted Robert's widow, parents and grandparents. One Amish man held Robert's sobbing father in his arms, reportedly for an hour, to comfort him. They set up a charitable fund for his family and attended his funeral. That is what made the evening news in the days that followed this tragedy. That is what we remember. Forgiveness was the only way to bring healing to that devastated community. So they forgave.

Forgiveness is not to be confused with leniency, with letting an abuser off the hook like nothing happened. But it has everything to do with respecting his human dignity. He cannot be free to continue his abuse, so, as indicated, incarceration may be called for, or other methods of restricting his activity if imprisonment is not imposed. In either case, he still has value as a child of God, brother priest and member of the Body of Christ. We do what we need to do to keep our society safe, but not at the expense of compromising the standards of human respect that make our society humane. I hope we still believe in redemption. Frankly, when we love in the spirit of Jesus we shouldn't have to worry about what others think. Yes, some will accuse us of being weak, but, as long as our bishops have done all in their power to assist the abused and to keep the vulnerable safe, I would like to think that then they would somehow witness to the mercy of God toward such offenders.

But what about those non-pedophiles, ordinary priests, who, through a moment of weakness or bad judgment, crossed some boundary, and for that act alone have been summarily removed from ministry as unworthy of the priesthood? That is even more disturbing. The Amish took that most difficult, necessary step toward the healing of their community, and with that step, hope was born for the future. It is a step that our married couples know they have to take if they are to move into the future with hope. I believe it is the church's next step, too, that is if we truly want to heal before we move on.

As we've said, The Dallas Charter stopped the bleeding, but it didn't bring healing. No one can afford to sit back and say, *"The job is done, so let's move on."* There is much to be done in the area of healing and reconciliation. A tourniquet is an emergency measure that must be followed up with good medical care if an arm is to be saved. But if it is left on too long, it could do irreparable damage. Rather than tighten down more, it may be time to take the next steps in the healing process. I'm not sure what those steps will look like, but things can't remain as they are. Ironically, a lack of trust is the issue, but it goes both ways. Our couples living the Sacrament of Matrimony may give a clue as to what those steps might be. They are certainly inviting those in leadership positions to act out of love and forgiveness. They know that that is the only way that good can overcome the evil in the current situation. It is incumbent on us as a church to learn this lesson. This should not come as a surprise!

* * * * * * *

Who is worthy to be a priest? No one, really. We all fall short, some more than others. It is interesting, though, that according to some of my Irish friends, the most popular priest confessors in Ireland are recovering alcoholics. When I first heard this, it came as a surprise. But the more I reflected on it, the more it made good sense. Apparently, rather than being scandalized by their weakness, the faithful believe that a wounded confessor will better understand them in their weakness than the confessor who shows no sign of human weakness. Fortunately, these good priests were given a second chance.

In this regard, Jesus was not surprised by our human weakness; in fact, he took advantage of it. The timing of Jesus' bestowing the power to forgive sins wasn't accidental. It was Easter Sunday night when Jesus chose to appear to the apostles who they were gathered in the upper room, huddling together more out of fear than anything else. Not only were they afraid of what the religious or civil authorities might do if they found them, I can also imagine they were anxious about what Jesus might say to them, that is, if the extraordinary news was true that he had risen from the dead. After all, Peter had three times denied even knowing who Jesus was and the rest had run away and hid in the shadows. It's not hard to imagine that, at a minimum, they figured they deserved a tongue lashing from Jesus.

But when Jesus appears to them, he doesn't say, *"I told you so."* Rather, he says, *"Peace be with you."* He invites them back into the flow of divine love so they can live life again. Then, at this crucial moment when they are most aware of their own failure and sinfulness, Jesus breathes on them and says, *"Receive the Holy Spirit. Whose sins you forgive are forgiven them...."* (John 20:23). It is as if Jesus is saying to them,

> *"I am giving to the Church the Holy Spirit, my Spirit, with the power to forgive sin. Use it wisely and generously. Remember, you are a sinner yourself! Never be stingy with my mercy! My forgiveness of you tonight is a total and complete gift. You did nothing to earn it. Therefore, you will forgive, not because the sinner before you is worthy, but because you share in the Spirit of God who is all merciful. You know what merciful love is because you have just experienced it, and you know the joy and peace that come from it. Be merciful, then, because I am merciful to you. Make mercy real in our world. And don't forget, from now on you will represent me, making my loving mercy present and believable in the world."*

I realize that our bishops are in extremely difficult positions when dealing with inappropriate behavior by any of their flock, especially priests. And they have to send the message that the church's moral teachings are not to be taken lightly. At times that can be done under the heading of tough love, but that would seem to be a last resort, since, as shepherds who go after the one sheep that goes astray, they must also send the message that genuine love is shown for the priest or lay person who strays, regardless of the disciplinary action taken. Improper religious behavior by them in violating some boundary is no more unacceptable than the improper religious behavior of failing to show compassion by those in authority. Their power must be tempered by love.

It is helpful for us also to reflect on the story of the woman caught in adultery in John's account of the gospel. While the scene is filled with drama, as the guilty woman's life is in the balance, Jesus turns the tables on the self righteous men who want to trap him in a situation where law vs. mercy. It is a cunning trap, and they're sure they have him. Then Jesus calls their bluff and says, *"Whoever is without sin, let him cast the first stone."* They walk away, beginning with the eldest. This story should serve as a constant reminder to any priest or bishop who has faculties to forgive sin in the name of the church. Their job is to express the mind and heart of Jesus who didn't allow his compassion to be trumped by the law.

The most remarkable thing about Jesus' extraordinary behavior during his passion that speaks to me and to our world today is not his silence, strength or surrender to the Father. It is this: Even though he was clearly a victim, Jesus never played the role of a victim, and he never created a victim. All he said was, *"Father, forgive them for they know not what they do"* (Father Richard Rohr). To those who really get it, that is what love looks like when everything is on the table. We have had people in history who have followed that path and have become famous, often as martyrs. But ordinary people do it everyday and don't become famous at all, and I'm speaking especially of husbands and wives, moms and dads. A woman told me how people assumed she would divorce her husband who had to serve time in jail. *"The thought never crossed my mind,"* she said. *"I loved him."* She could have played the role of a victim and victimized her husband and children, but she didn't. Instead, she loved her husband and forgave him. They are still happily married, and their kids still have a mother and father who love each other.

Sadly, there are times when parents are victimized by their children. But most parents never play the role of a victim. I've been with them when they cry in sadness and grief, especially should their child have to serve time in jail. But I've seldom heard any of them say, *"Poor me."* They take whatever it is that is thrown at them still loving their children the whole while. And the last thing they want to do is to victimize their child. They know it will only make things worse. In our society, I don't know of anyone else who expresses the spirit of Jesus better. *"Love bears all things"* (1Cor. 13:7).

Again, our couples show what the depth of love looks like. They take their cue from Jesus, although they probably don't realize it. When we study Jesus in the gospel, we see that when compassion comes in conflict with the law, Jesus consistently comes down on the side of compassion. Even when justice demands that a child must pay the penalty of the law, a parent's compassion is not compromised. That may just be because that is the nature of genuine love and what it does when it hurts so much. They are learning the ways of love in ways they neither wanted nor imagined.

Granted, in the heat of conflict and the pain of hurt, it is easy to be blinded to the goodness of the one who violated them and their trust. It hurts also because the person's sin may reflect negatively on the family or on them as parents. I think it is unavoidable as it goes with the risk of loving the members of your family. Granted, this hurt may be used as an excuse for coming down hard and rejecting a child, but it is not a legitimate reason. Goodness is still there even when it has been momentarily overwhelmed by bad behavior. I think that the only eyes that can see that goodness when no one else can see it are the eyes of love. We can't forget that when we love in the spirit of Jesus, we love goodness into the ones we love.

The reason I believe this is because I've seen our sacramental couples love each other and the members of their families this way, with agape love. And agape love sees goodness, not evil. It is compassionate, not vindictive. It forgives, rather than broods. It seeks healing, not revenge. As Fr. Robert Spitzer, S.J. once said at the Los Angeles Religious Education Congress, *"Agape love is the salvation of human culture."* How? Because it is the only love that recognizes fully the dignity of the human person. And if we don't recognize that, our culture is doomed. To this I add, who are better poised to proclaim by word and action the power of agape love than our sacramental couples who vowed to love as Jesus loves us? To use the pearl theme: "This is why they are precious gems in the treasury of the church." We can no longer afford to ignore them.

We are facing some very serious issues in our church and world today. It is easy to lose hope; to give up or to give in. But our couples say to me by their lives that there is a better way to meet these challenges. When they live the dignity of their sacramental calling their message is like a herald's trumpet calling us to hope. They point us to the way of Jesus, to the way of merciful love. And for this reason, I see our couples as extraordinary bearers of hope in our church. For without their witness, which can be prophetic at times, I don't see how the church can be a sign of hope to anyone!

When we drift away from healthy relationships with one another, they call us back. After all, hope must happen in our hearts if there is ever to be hope for our world. Hope is the work of the Spirit. And it is that Spirit that enables us to see with the eyes of love, and in that seeing we will see all things new. Truly, our sacramental couples deserve our gratitude for loving each other so well for so long day after day, year after year even when it is hard; and we should not hesitate to thank them.

CONVERSATION STARTERS:

1. Why is forgiveness and reconciliation so critical to a marital relationship?

2. What might you as a wounded couple have to offer the Church?

3. Why is faith needed to live the Sacrament of Matrimony?

4. If the issue isn't worthiness, what is it?

5. Is admitting one's weakness a weakness?

---

1. Ron Rolheiser, *The Holy Longing,* (Doubleday, New York, 1999), p. 88

2. *Meditations on the Song of Songs,* The Collected Works of St. Teresa of Avila; ICS Publications

CHAPTER EIGHT

A CALL TO UNITY

"You mean I have to dance with everyone?"

The doctor said to the man after his physical, *"My, you're in great shape for a guy who's 60 years old."* *"Who said I was 60?"* the man countered. *"I was 80 my last birthday."* The doctor was amazed and said, *"How old was your father when he died?"* *"Who said my father died? He's a 104."* *"You're kidding,"* the doctor said. *"Well how old was your grandfather when he died?"* *"Who said my grandfather died? He's 129. In fact, he's getting married next week."* Flabbergasted, the doctor asked, *"Why would a guy 129 years old want to get married?"* *"Who said he wanted to get married?"*

* * * * * * *

We have to be careful about the assumptions we make. What may seem obvious to us may not be true at all. If we are not careful, we could start making judgments that could get us into trouble. It's not that we are bad or evil, but just that we are wounded by that sin of Adam. As the story is told, we suffer the effects of his having eaten from the Tree of Knowledge of Good and Evil. The sad evidence of history indicates that mankind has apparently acquired a taste for evil and, for the most part, doesn't realize it. In fact, it is a little scary. How much suffering and pain have been inflicted on the world by people who were convinced they were right? I'd say most of it.

It's sort of like the Humpty-Dumpty story all over again. The unity of creation intended by God from the beginning, "fell off the wall" when Adam and Eve sinned. Overcoming the effects of the fall has been the struggle ever since. The work of putting creation back together again began in earnest with the story of Abraham when God intervened into our history to initiate the long process. He formed a people he could call his own and gave it leaders, kings and prophets, (all the king's horses and all the king's men) but they couldn't put it back together again. And so, to make a very long story short, about 2,000 years ago, to the utter astonishment of everyone, that divine, creative, healing, redemptive love we call God was enfleshed in the one we know as Jesus of Nazareth. His life made it clear that the ultimate goal of that reconciliation process was to call us back to where we had begun, back "home" as it were, that is, to a life lived in the eternal flow of divine love (grace). He would himself be the way to unity, the only one who could put us back together again.

In Jesus, we could now see what divine love looked like when lived out in the human condition. Of course, it ultimately led to the cross. But we discover that love is even stronger than death, as the tomb could simply not contain him. Jesus then sends the Holy Spirit of his love into the believing hearts of his disciples so that the work he had began would continue through them. And what is that work? It is the work of reconciliation (2 Corinthians 5:18-21), of bringing people together, of healing broken relationships *"... that we might be one so the world may believe."* And, while this is the work of the whole church, my awareness of the power of the Sacrament of Matrimony is convincing me that our couples can have a crucial role to play in this effort.

The sacred bond between a Christian man and a Christian woman is above all a relationship of love that is wonderfully interwoven with the flow of divine love. As a sign of the mystery of the church herself, they long for unity in the Spirit of God's love. They give life and they give it in abundance because God is present in their love relationship. And to add to the wonder of it all, our couples call their brothers and sisters in the faith to a depth of love in their relationships with one another in the church. They help us recognize what genuine love looks like in the here and now everyday struggles of living life. And even when that way to unity is not clearly understood, they reveal the church's inner-longing to keep trying to find that way.

So, this leads us back to our fundamental thesis. We are on this earth to learn how to love. Our most important task as human beings is to learn the ways of love, and, of course, to pass them on. But now we know why. Love and love alone has the power to mend the breaches between people and lead to the kind of unity that gives credibility to the teaching of the church. *"... that they all may be one as you, Father, are in me and I am in you, that they may also be one in us that the world may believe you sent me" (John 17:21).* After all, deep down, isn't that what the church is for? In the church, unity among diverse people is possible through the Holy Spirit. That is what draws people to us, and through us to Jesus! So goes the theory.

* * * * * * *

But things happen that we don't expect that throw us off our game, even in the most "peaceful" of families. For example, what child growing up with brothers and sisters hasn't heard a parent say, *"If you kids don't stop fighting, I'll stop the car and make you walk!"* My brothers and I heard it more than once. There is something about siblings who sit next to each other in a car that leads to conflict. *"Quit touching me!"* *"Mom, make him stop looking at me!"* You know the routine. In their own way, parents become experts at anger management. While all they really want is peace and quiet, the underlying truth is that they want unity in their families. That sensitivity should speak to us in the family of the church that seems to find so many things to fight over.

As one person observed, *"What area of church life isn't controversial?"* Take your pick: the liturgy, the role of women, celibacy, Vatican II, the Latin Mass, the ringing of bells, or the non-ringing of bells. While most of these are pretty manageable, some can get out of control and lead to actual polarization in the church. People pick sides and pretty soon it becomes an "us" against "them" situation. This, of course, interrupts the steady flow of love between the members of the church. The left (liberal, Vatican II, progressive, take your pick) is suspicious of the right (conservative, pre-Vatican II, traditional, take your pick). At the same time, the right is suspicious of the left, which leads to camps of one against the other, again setting the stage for outright distrust and conflict. When this happens, love seems to go into hiding. Granted, there will be two or more sides to all issues, but that doesn't mean there has to be rancor going on between the sides. (Obviously, I'm referring to conditions in the Roman Catholic Church only.)

Since this is fundamentally a relationship issue, the question we have to ask is what is this polarization doing to us? That is the main thing. The issue isn't really who is right and who is wrong. I know some couples who disagree vehemently over politics. They cancel out each other's vote every election, but they still love each other. They continue to raise their children, go to work and have fun together. They choose to agree to disagree, although they are probably both praying for God's mercy on the other.

When a pastor is caught in the tension between his parishioners, he would be wise to learn what married couples learned along the way, that when one side tries to win by dominating the other, both sides lose. Couples who know how to fight fairly will ultimately fight for the sake of their relationship. There has to be a way to find common ground and then expand on that. Of course, they can always agree to disagree. We also have to find a way to stop demonizing those who disagree with us, a form of criticism that is particularly damaging. I believe this will take some truly courageous, wise and inspired leadership in the church.

What is happening to us is painful to watch. However, our couples remind us that we can't just ignore a problem where one exists. That will only make things worse. I've met many a husband whose wife finally walked out on him because he refused to listen to her and simply ignored that he had a problem with drinking, or gambling, or being married to his job, or whatever. The act of her walking out finally got his attention enough to motivate him to seek help, but by then it was often too late to do anything about it. Couples have learned the hard way that whatever the issue is, it just won't go away. It needs to be addressed.

Savvy couples know that it does no good for one to say, *"I don't want to talk about it,"* as if that were a solution. For one thing, it disregards legitimate concerns the other may have. Trying to silence one's spouse doesn't work any better. It just indicates the desire to dominate, even suppress the other, thus showing a lack of respect for the other's goodness and dignity, and can hardly be held up as an example of what genuine love looks like. Quite frankly, telling someone to "shut up!" often betrays a possible weakness in one's own position. When I was a pastor, the last thing I wanted to do was to pull rank to get my way. That may be the way that raw power operates, but not loving power. Yet, these tactics are all alive and well in the church. I think we have a lot to learn, and we can learn much of it from our surprising couples.

Our sacramental couples again remind us that a serious issue may be the collateral damage that this polarization is inflicting on us as the Body of Christ. I put it this way because innocent bystanders, like the children of couples in conflict, are often injured by what is going on between the one's they look up to. Open conflict can weaken the unity that is called for in both a marriage and in a church community. And the more factions that develop in the church, the more we drift away from the unity Jesus wanted for us when he prayed at the Last Supper, *"May they be one, Father, ..."* (John 17: 21). This compromises all the more the power of the gospel to touch the hearts of those who turn to the church for direction and meaning in their lives.

Like the couple who came to realize that the state of marriage is much bigger than they are and their personal relationship, the leaders of the church, self included, must realize that we are about something far bigger than our personal preferences, likes and dislikes. It is not about me, but us. We need to keep asking ourselves if what we are doing is compatible with the gospel of Jesus. Does it further the credibility of the gospel? Is it life-giving to our people? Does it respect the *"sensus fidelium,"* that is, the faith of the faithful? Will it help bring unity to the church? What will give the most glory to God?

In families, parents instinctively know that they can't favor one child over another. They may love them differently, but just as much. Similarly, we priests need to know that we cannot just play to one segment of the church at the expense of another. If we do, we are, in effect, dividing the church. I personally do not take it as sign of health when a parish is hailed for being very conservative or very liberal. Both could well be ignoring a segment of parishioners who need to be respected and ministered to. In effect, it sends the message that some people are not all that welcome, as in, *"If you don't like it, go someplace else."* While St. Paul's idea of *"being all things to all people"* isn't realistic for us who are so flawed, it does remind us that everyone in our parishes should be important to us. Rather than specialists, parish priests should be more like general practitioners, interested in anyone who knocks on our door.

This reminds me of the Saturday morning in June about 11 o'clock when the rectory doorbell rang. I quickly looked out the window and saw a large number of cars in the parking lot. *"Don't tell me I forgot a wedding?!"* I said to myself. I went to the door fully expecting to see a best man in tux ready to inform me that the church was full of people waiting for me. I opened the door and there, standing before me, was a bum wanting a handout. *"Boy am I glad to see you!"* I said to him. *"What do you want?"*

Isn't it ironic that those on the extreme right and extreme left are really very much alike? Neither is truly inclined to welcome all who come. They can both be quite selective of the people they choose to embrace. To the degree either is exclusive, to that degree they are not truly catholic (universal) in spirit. A priest I knew years ago was very conservative in church matters, very dogmatic in his opinions. Then he was sent to a pastor that was more authoritarian than he, and he got hurt. He then became very liberal, but he was just as dogmatic about his liberal opinions as he had been before about his conservative opinions. He hadn't really changed at all. He just changed sides.

It is the work of the Spirit to unite, not divide. I don't see how we can cater just to that segment of the church that agrees with our way of doing things. It will demand the very best we have to offer as pastors to unite the factions in a parish. Our first task is to keep those at odds with each other from mutual destruction and then try to lead them to common ground; to help them see that what unites us is more important than what divides us. If you will, the "main thing" about the Church's existence is to further the kingdom of God. And that is impossible to do if we do not build around the divine, transcendental qualities of one, true, good and beautiful. While they will never be totally within our reach on this earth, they do keep us moving in the right direction.

Whether we liked it or not, most bishops, priests and lay leaders that I know from my era worked hard and in good faith to implement the teachings of the Second Vatican Council, often learning as we made our way. Some arguably silly things done early on were by-in-large corrected over the years. Among other things, believing in the significance of collegiality and more open communications, we looked forward to the updating of liturgical texts that would express the beauty and depth of our official prayers and show their inclusive nature. We trusted and believed that it was the work of the Holy Spirit that Pope John XXIII prayed for in that extraordinary time of *aggiornamento*.

Then, inexplicably, began the so-called "reform of the reform." It's as if the Holy Spirit suddenly changed its mind, saying a few years ago, *"Oh gosh, I must have made a mistake."* It is as though someone was trying to put the new wine of Vatican II into old wine skins of another time, although Jesus warned us that doing such things would not be all that wise. Eventually, something is probably going to burst. But we're doing it anyway. The church, as the Body of Christ, is a living institution and is bound to change whether we like it or not. For many priests, self included again, this "reform of the reform" is a discouraging development. Those in control were committed to control! While some in the church are celebrating, others are mourning. We are divided

> *"Knock! Knock!"*
> *"Who's there?"*
> *"A controller. Now this is where you say, 'A controller who?"....*

Using the paradigm of the Paschal Mystery, Father Ron Rolheiser, O.M.I. has a wonderful insight that has helped me deal with people in mourning, and could help me in dealing with this.[1] It can also say something to both those who have resisted Vatican II for the last 50 years and to those who mourn its apparent "passing" today.

When Mary Magdalene saw the risen Jesus on Easter morning, she wanted to embrace him. Jesus stopped her, saying in effect, *"You cannot approach me as before. Things are different now. Yes, I live, and we will have a future, but it will not be the same."* Then, as Rolheiser explains it, Mary has forty days to mourn what used to be. Come the Ascension, she would have to let go of Jesus as she had known him. And in that letting go, she enabled her heart to open to the coming Pentecost and the gift of the Holy Spirit who would both fill and guide her into new ways of life unknown to her. Letting go is critical to the healing process.

Two stories: #1 An acquaintance of mine lost her husband to a massive heart attack while he was out walking. Of course, she was distraught, but she apparently never got over it. Years after the event, I went to visit her and the shades of her house were closed in mid afternoon. She was still in mourning. Living in denial, it seems that she still, somehow, had expected her husband to walk through the front door. She hadn't let him go, and that closed her to the Spirit and to a future of new possibilities.

#2 A couple lost their two year old son in a drowning incident. Both were devastated. It was as if their world had collapsed around them. It was difficult for them to go on. (It is said that about 80% of couples who lose a child end up divorcing.) The future seemed pointless. While they had been to a professional counselor, at the suggestion of relatives in our parish, they also came to see me. I told them the Mary Magdalene story. I wouldn't be surprised if their "40 days of mourning" didn't last well over a year. I lost track of them for some time, but when I saw them again, the mother was holding a newborn baby girl. She and her husband finally came to the point where they could both let their son go to his Heavenly Father, and it opened them to the Holy Spirit and to what the future might bring. Each story holds important lessons for us to learn.

* * * * * * *

Could our couples have anything to say about the growing phenomenon of individualism in our society and church? It is a way of life that centers on the selfish, little trinity of "me, myself and I." Well, what parent doesn't have to deal with this when their children go through their mid and late teens? I've had many a wedding where the young couples getting married are just beginning to break out of "the-world-revolves-around-me" phase of their lives. It is the first real challenge some of them will have to face. They need to learn that marriage is not about "me," but "us," not doing it "my way" but "our way." Fortunately, God has given married couples a wonderful way to come to realize it is about two, not one (and then three and more). The passion of love, the excitement of everything new, all build an aura of blissful joy that gives rise to that fairytale ending, *"and they lived happily ever after."* Honeymoons serve a great purpose, but, unlike fairytale endings, they don't last forever.

Of course, the "me" inevitably surfaces again when their idyllic joy is threatened by those predictable signs of selfishness; those thoughtless slights, missed compliments, negative non-verbal messages, disagreements on how things should be done, tactless insensitivities, and previously unseen weaknesses. What was once considered cute in the other while dating now bugs the hell out of them. Some couples may begin to wonder if they made a mistake to get married in the first place. But they remember their vows, *"for better or worse,"* so they stay with it. They may have heard that being a husband is to be about the wife, and being a wife is to be about her husband. So they hang in there and face their demons and forgive and surrender and serve and thereby grow in the ways of love they never dreamed of. Over time, they learn to embrace each other in both their struggles and weaknesses, and that's what enables them to stay for the long haul, to mature, and to grow together in the ways of love.

The priesthood and Christianity itself is not about "me" and "my way" either. It's about us. It's about fidelity to our baptismal promises (vows). It's about dealing with broken people, and forgiving and surrendering and serving and embracing people with weaknesses. New converts to the church as well as some newly ordained priests are much like couples on honeymoons. They can't imagine everything not being perfect. But there comes a time when the fragrance of the Sacred Chrism fades away and they realize that they are no longer the center of attention as neophytes and new priests; then it becomes obvious that the people of the church are flawed, including themselves. Some may begin to wonder if they did the right thing to accept Baptism or to receive the Sacrament of Orders.

But, with a little effort, they realize it is still possible to learn the ways of love within the limitations of an imperfect church. Since the Eucharist is to the community of faith what sexual intimacy is to the married couple, it sustains them through difficult times. It is our communion, not only with Jesus in the Host, but also with the Jesus of the other Body of Christ, the church, that holds us together in spite of ourselves.

* * * * * * *

This leads to another issue in the church. For some people, it is hard to accept the fact that the church is made up of flawed people, including their priests. Some of these people deputize themselves as members of the so-called "orthodoxy police." Every parish has someone who wants to make sure the priest doesn't break any rules and is faithful to the teaching of the Holy Father in every detail as they define them. I've heard that many of these people, though not all of course, are often new to the church, or may have recently returned to the church after having been away for sometime. They now totally embrace the laws they never understood or just ignored before; realizing at last that their earlier disobedience often led to their former way of life and the messes it got them into. With their new awakening of faith, the law now becomes everything.

I see similarities between the "orthodoxy police" and those in a family we used to call "tattletales." When a little sister sees a big brother do something wrong she has to go tell their mother. We're not talking major offences here, like abuse of children or anything like that, but smaller things, even picky things. The tattler is often quite self-righteous about it all. In the gospels, they are the ones who watched Jesus closely with the hope of catching him in some violation of the law. They did this, not because they were so holy and pure themselves, as Jesus masterfully pointed out on more than one occasion, but because Jesus was seen as a threat to them in some way. As we might say today, *"They wanted to stick it to him."*

To a savvy mother, the tattletale child is often as much a concern as the big brother. Since tattling is not an act of love, she'll listen to the complaint, but not act on it the way the little sister wants, which is to get her big brother into trouble. Mom might end up saying something to the big brother, but not in a way that gives a sense of victory to the tattletale. She might even tell her to grow up, or do something about it herself. Among other things, she wants to teach her child to take responsibility for her actions and not expect someone else to fight her battles.

The most effective response I've seen when a priest is turned in to the bishop for some minor thing is when the bishop tells the person to go talk to the priest himself. What bothers the priest is when the bishop takes the accusation of the "orthodoxy police" as objective and reprimands the priest on their word alone. Such a response can easily be translated in the priest's mind as a lack of support, indicating the bishop's lack of faith in him. It breeds distrust and drains energy. If there is need for some corrective action, it can be done without embarrassing the priest before his people.

I've heard people on Catholic radio encourage listeners to check up on their priests to make sure they were faithfully obeying the liturgical norms, thus practically deputizing them as the "liturgy police." I heard one caller complain to the talk show host about his pastor who began a Eucharistic Prayer with the words of institution. The host told him the priest shouldn't be doing that, never alluding to the fact that the priest was probably using Eucharistic Prayer II that practically begins with the words of institution. He should have known better.

One time during confession, the penitent asked me right out, *"Do you believe that you have the power to forgive sin?"* I couldn't believe my ears. *"Where did that come from?"* I wondered. Was he actually suspicious of my faith in the sacrament I was celebrating? All I said was, *"I've been hearing confessions for over 47 years. No one even asked me that before.*

Do you think I'd be doing this if I didn't believe people walked out of here forgiven?" But he persisted, *"But do you believe you forgave them?"* The tone of his voice made it clear that he was giving me a test. But a good answer called for more than a "yes" or "no" from me, and I had neither the time nor desire to give him a lesson in sacramental theology and how Christ acts through the sacraments. If a little knowledge is a dangerous thing, then being challenged by "cocksure ignorance" is truly scary.

I felt sad for him and also for our church if it is coming to this. Such self-appointed "protectors of the faith" often want to "out Catholic" life-long Catholics. It's sort of like newly weds wanting to tell their grandparents what marriage is all about. The ones I fault most are those who encourage them to be suspicious. It is hard to feel believed in when your people question your every move. Fortunately, this hasn't happened to me very often. Maybe they're looking for the perfect pastor. Now, if their pastor is looking for the perfect parishioner, they'd both be in trouble. Isn't it fun!

But when we have experienced our brokenness as a church - and those of us who have been around awhile have - we can still remain faithful to our baptismal vows, our confirmation and ordination, deeply love the Church and still cut ourselves and others a little slack for not doing everything perfectly by the book. And furthermore, even if we do everything by the book, it's no guarantee we are doing everything with love, and that is what matters most. Maybe this is where we need to be reminded that *"Love covers a multitude of sins."* (1 Peter 4:8) or *"The letter kills but the Spirit gives life"* (2 Corinthians. 3:7).

Speaking of Catholic radio, which I believe is in many ways is a true gift to the church, it may, nonetheless, contribute to the division in the church. For example, it irritates me no end when I hear someone identify newly ordained priests as the "good priests," implying that older priests are "bad priests." As an older priest, or "senior priest" if you will, I resent that kind of talk. It is both silly and arrogant, not to mention divisive.

At a recent gathering of the priests of our archdiocese, I looked around the room and said to myself, *"Pound for pound, I don't think I could claim a better group of men to have as my colleagues. Some of us are a little odd, but when did it become a sin to be a little odd? I am truly blessed to have been a part of this presbyterate for 50 years."* And that blessing extends to our bishops. I remember one bishop getting very angry with me over something I had done. In plain words, he reamed me out, and he had a right to. But the next time I saw him, it was like nothing had ever happened. I learned that you can disagree with someone and still respect them at the same time. This is why the categories of "good priest" and "bad priest" never entered our minds back then. We were just priests. I fear we may be losing that mutual respect in today's church. I hope not.

We hear of "Vatican II" priests and "John Paul II" priests. Again, to think one is better than the other is foolish. It echoes the scandal St. Paul had to address in Corinth when some said they followed Paul, others Apollos, some Cephas and others Christ (1 Cor. 1:12). We all share in the same priesthood, as ultimately there is only one priest, Jesus. To identify ourselves with a time in history or a person of history, as innocent as it may seem, is to miss the point. Priests of my era tried to be as Christ-like as we knew how in our time, and the same is expected of priests today. That is the challenge we all face, and we all fall short. We need to remember that it is not about us and who we are anyway. It never is. We are about being priests of Jesus Christ in the time we have to serve the church as priests, and it's not very long. To glory in anything else is an embarrassment to the priesthood and a disservice to our people.

The issue isn't liberal vs. conservative, young vs. old, or whatever. It is our unity as a presbyterate, a unity that is born of the Spirit we got caught up in when we were ordained; it's another gift. I recall one of our priests who left active ministry, I think because of a drinking problem and some other issues he was dealing with. He ended up on the streets of Seattle, living alone in a small, run down apartment. At his funeral Mass, I found out that he spent the last years of his life ministering to the down and out men and woman who also lived on the streets with him. I feel blessed to have had him as a brother priest. Deep down, he, too, was a good priest, maybe even a very holy priest. He had a desire to please God, and that kept him going till the day he died.

* * * * * * *

Let me ask a question. Who loves each other more, a couple returning from their honeymoon, or a couple celebrating their 50th wedding anniversary? With the young couple, everything is fresh, wonderful, exciting and even innocent. And with the old couple? Let's just say there is no way they can go back to the joys of their honeymoon. They know too much. But now they lovingly embrace each other in the full knowledge of each other's limitations, having given and received forgiveness from each other 70 x 7 times. They have learned that life isn't simple and, because it isn't, it taught them the tough lessons of love. While a newly married couple has important gifts to bring to the church, I'll put my money on the old folks.

> A minister had a meeting of his men's club. In the course of it he asked the men how long they had been married. *"Ten years,"* said one; *"17 years,"* said another, *"33 years,"* said a third. Then Oly raised his hand. *"And how long have you been married Oly?"* the minister asked. *"50 years to Lena next month." "That's wonderful,"* remarked the minister, *"and to what do you attribute the longevity of your marriage?" "Vell,"* said Oly, *"Lena and I took a trip to Norvay for our 25th wedding anniversary." "What a wonderful thing to do,"* commented the minister. *"What are you going to do for your 50th?" "I'm going back to get 'er."* answered Oly,

Of course, married couples can teach us about one obvious area of friction in the church that we could easily miss. It comes from the fact that there are men and women who truly love each other. I get the impression from listening to some angry people that such a thing is impossible. *"Love a man? You have to be kidding. Who needs them? Who wants them?"*... *"Love a woman? Are you insane?"* To the degree that there is distrust of women by the men of the church, and of men by women of the church, to that degree the stage is set for discord between the two.

Men and women both need to pay attention to our married couples. Rather than try to resolve their issues out of fear and suspicion, they work out of mutual love. When they fight, they fight ultimately for their relationship. There is no place for domination one over the other. If St. Paul is right, it is *"love that conquers all things,"* nothing else. In the spirit of the Ascension, maybe both men and women need to ask what it is that they are afraid of letting go of to be open to the Spirit and to the future.

I must add that, in all honesty, the playing field is not level. Since men are in the positions of power, they have the greater responsibility to try to resolve this tension. Do we need to be reminded that Jesus exercised his power by saving the life of the woman caught in adultery, by respecting the dignity of the Samaritan woman at the well and by praising the courage of the Canaanite woman who outsmarted him (Matt. 15: 21-28); and by allowing Mary of Bethany to sit at his feet as a learner, which women simply didn't do, while Martha fussed; or how he let the sinful woman wash his feet because she saw what no one else could see? It does not bode well when I visit parishes where girls are excluded from being altar servers. Of course, their pastors are convinced they are doing the right thing. While they're looking for priestly vocations, the girls feel discrimination.

In some situations, what love should look like is almost impossible to know. It is not clear what will bring healing to a family, such as when parents see that their older children are no longer speaking to each other. While they don't know what to do to stop the pain of it all, they are not indifferent to it, either. Even in cases when a child has drifted away from both family and faith, I'd bet that parents seldom if ever speak of that child as bad, but rather as a *"good kid who made some bad decisions,"* or *"one who just got in with the wrong crowd."* The love in their eyes sees goodness in spite of the child's flaws and personal problems.

Whether or not this parental evaluation is more optimistic than accurate, the important thing about it is that it keeps the door of their hearts open to reconciliation someday. I believe our sacramental couples have insights into the way relationships work, and could help the church overcome its present polarized condition. If nothing else, they should make us feel uncomfortable the longer we tolerate our obvious lack of unity.

Anthony Padovano has a wonderful description of home in one of his writings. He said something to this effect: *"Home is not so much a place as it is an attitude; a condition of mind and heart. Home is where we want to live; where we are at peace. Home is being free to be ourselves with the people in our lives who love us the way we are. To be home is to say, 'I don't want to be somewhere else or someone else.'"* This doesn't just happen, nor does it require wealth, status or privilege. It only requires people who live the way of love, where each person is respected and valued in keeping with their human dignity. "Home" is the byproduct of close, loving, family relationships. When I went to college out of state, I experienced the real pain of being homesick, which I now regard as healthy evidence that I had come from a loving home.

* * * * * * *

The sad thing today is that our Catholic couples by-in-large have no idea just how magnificent their vocation is as sacraments of the church. At best, they have only a vague awareness that they have a vocation from God at all. The fact that it has a crucial role to play in God's Plan for the well being of the church and our society never entered their heads.

This has to change. More is riding on the renewal of the Sacrament of Matrimony in the church than just getting more young people to have their weddings in the church. We, the church, need the movement of the Spirit in our midst. To a great extent, that Spirit will be with us through the loving relationships of our couples. They bring the power of love to bear upon our communities, enlivening them, and even transforming them bit by bit into communities where we, its members, will be known by our love for one another.

While we have spent a great deal of time looking at the ways we need the grace of the Sacrament of Matrimony to address many of the problems facing the church, we need it even more to bring the power of love to work as a leaven in our church community. Even if there were no problems in the church, the Sacrament of Matrimony still would be an important factor in its general spirit and life. All couples, not just those struggling with their relationships, need the encouragement that comes from hearing other couples tell their stories. This is why small sharing groups of married couples are so important to the life of a parish. I am in no way opposed to nor do I discourage other small faith communities that gather and share their life and faith experiences. But if our couples are not gathering to share their life and faith journeys <u>as married couples</u>, something very important would be missing in a parish.

The family, which Pope Paul VI called the "little church," is to the "big church" what the "big church" is to the world. As the family is a leaven in the dough of our church, the family of the church is to be a leaven in the dough of our culture. The family must be a sign of hope in a church and world where marriage has lost its center, its meaning, its significance for the health and well being of our society. Our families have to show that true human fulfillment cannot be bought by amassing wealth, acquired by gaining power, or secured by conquering our enemies. Human fulfillment comes from living a way of life that surrenders itself into the eternal flow of Divine Love that existed for all eternity, and continues to flow through our world today wherever love exists between people. And the family will be as strong as are those who lead them, our sacramental couples.

Whatever else people might get from reading the magazines on display at the checkout counter of their local supermarkets, they don't get much inspiration; a lot of scandal maybe, some intrigue for sure, and ample provocative images meant to stimulate their imagination, but not much inspiration. They don't inspire because they aren't the work of the Spirit. They seldom breathe new life into anything. Celebrities who are in their third, fourth or fifth marriage are not experts on marriage. They're experts on divorce. Yet, those who read these magazines are probably looking for something in their lives that is missing. I believe it was G.K. Chesterton who said, *"A man who goes to a brothel is really looking for God, but doesn't know it."*

The longing in our hearts is a good thing, not bad. As Norman Langenbrunner says in my good old **Weekday Homily Helps,** *"There is something in us that always wants more. Even if we fulfill a dream or acquire a possession we've always wanted, we soon discover it is insufficient to completely satisfy us. Some may consider this ongoing hunger for more a curse; God considers it a homing device or a magnetic pull designed to bring us to him."* [2] If God created us to enter into the mystery of divine life, there will always be something lacking in our lives until we enter it. And since grace is the love of God "outside of God," there is nothing more important for us than to live in God's grace, to live in the ever flowing stream of divine love. It alone can satisfy the deepest longings of the human heart. Only when we are living in union with God (living in love), are we giving glory to God. Then we will be living as God created us to live. After all, that is what gives glory to God.

Trees give glory to God by being trees, dogs by being dogs, cats by being cats (although this is a stretch), and humans by being human, nothing more and nothing less. If, as St. Irenaeus said in the second century, *"The glory of God is the human person fully alive,"* then we can see that God desires, longs for us to live life to the full. And since God is love, the more we live in love, the closer we will come to living life to the full. Our goal in life is clearly not just to avoid eternal punishment, but to give glory to God by living the commandment of love. When we do that, salvation will take care of itself.

* * * * * * *

It is worth repeating that our married couples didn't ask for any of this when they got married, mostly because they didn't know anything about it. They just wanted to love each other, raise a family together and spend the rest of their lives sharing each other's company. But what if they had known? What if they were aware of God's call to them to be sacraments of divine love to the church and ultimately to the world? It isn't that they would have had to live their lives all that differently, but it could have inspired them to live their lives with greater purpose, aware that their love for each other was also meant to touch the lives of countless others.

And what if they realized that the way they lived the new commandment of love was even crucial to those others? What if they were aware that God was counting on them to touch others in the Spirit of Jesus, especially with compassion and love? After all, that is their God-given vocation through the church. And what if they felt believed in by their bishops, pastors and other members of their faith communities? I can't help but think it would have made a big difference to them; to their self esteem as married couples, to their spiritual lives and to their sense of worth to the church. Rather than being like pawns on the ecclesial chess board, they'd have the dignity of rooks and knights, along with the bishops (and priests), to serve the King.

CONVERSATION STARTERS:

1. How do you find common ground when you have strong differences of opinion?

2. Does proving you are right bring healing to your relationship?

3. How do you deal with teens who have all the answers?

4. How important is mutual faith in a relationship? In the church?

5. Why is unity the goal of marriage, and not just getting along?

---

1. *Ron Rolheiser,* The Holy Longing, *(Doubleday, New York).* 1999, pp. 147 & 166.

2. *Weekday Homily Helps*: St. Anthony Messenger Press, Cincinnati, OH, October 3, 2009.

CHAPTER NINE

LITTLE THINGS MEAN A LOT

"Not to worry."

Standing on the first tee, he looks like a golfer, wearing a golf cap, knickers and argyle socks. He sets up for his first drive of the day trying to ignore the heavy woods to the right of the fairway. He does his little waggle and then hits the ball with great determination. He can't believe his eyes as it slices off toward the dreaded deep woods. *"I sure hope I can find that ball,"* he says to himself as he heads out after it. Sure enough, he finds the ball. Then he says, *"I sure hope I have a shot out of here so I don't have to take a penalty stroke."* Sure enough, he even sees something of a tunnel through the trees, and if he hits a low screamer, with a little luck, he could even roll the ball up onto the first green. So he takes careful aim and again strikes the ball with determination. It takes off too high, ricochets off a branch, comes back and hits him in the head and kills him dead. Suddenly, he appears before the pearly gates of heaven. St. Peter sees him and says to him, *"You look like a golfer."* *"I am,"* he says. *"Are you any good?"* asks St. Peter. *"Well, I got here in two."*

* * * * * * *

Life is a mysterious gift, and things don't always work out as planned. You know what they say about the best laid plans of mice and men. But sometimes, however, they work out better than planned. When things go right, it is every bit as much a mystery to me, especially in the world of golf. While the devil gets all the publicity for being in the details of our plans, I think angels are in there, too, quietly doing their good work without fanfare or credit. At least, that is what I like to believe. For me, a 210 yard drive down the middle of the fairway is as much a mystery as a slice into the woods. Who knows, maybe God's finger is somehow at work in the details of my swing, at least once in awhile. So why worry?

The way of life that is called for in the Sacrament of Matrimony takes it far beyond the range of anything we might call a program. It is about living in the Spirit of God's love as Catholic Christians in the context of the committed love relationship of a husband and wife. As far as the couple is concerned, when they make their vows on their wedding day, it doesn't matter to them where the future leads them as long as they can go together with the assurance that God is with them. And God promised to be with them always, to be a part of their lives, not apart from their lives. They tap into that divine presence when they live the ways of love. Sacramental marriage is a way of life that centers on the great mystery of love. So, whatever happens when love is given, received, or extended in whatever form, God is there, often unseen and unnoticed, that is, unless we have eyes to see and ears to hear.

Life is not easy because life is about loving in good times and bad; in little things and big. While the world is full of people living in good faith who sincerely want to live good and loving lives, I don't know how any of us can do that, or how we can really learn the challenging ways of love without believing in a God of love, specifically, without knowing Jesus Christ. He is the love that existed for all eternity that became one of us and dwelt with us in human form. By studying him and how he lived, we can see what the kind of love that we ultimately need to learn looks like if we want to live life to the full. Then we have to allow God's love to transform our hearts. In other words, any Catholic couple wanting to live their vocation as a sacrament in, of and for the church must take their Catholic faith seriously. There is no option.

Taking one's faith seriously is not a matter of memorizing the scriptures chapter and verse. It is not a matter of having religious art hanging on all the walls of our homes, or of wearing a religious medal around our neck, or praying the family Rosary every night as a family. It does not even mean one has to spend a holy hour everyday before the Blessed Sacrament. While each of these practices is commendable, and I encourage them, they are not what I have in mind. You see, we could do all of these things and still not take our Catholic faith seriously. That is to say, we could do all these things and not be very loving. When we chose to live the way of love that Jesus taught and lived, then we are taking our faith seriously.

I've seen too many families that are exceptionally "religious" with kids who can't wait to break free from it all. It should never be oppressive! True, faith must be in the air the children breathe while growing up, but that air shouldn't be stiflingly religious. There must be a gentle breeze of loving acceptance and joyful respect that is also in the air, sort of like the trade winds in Hawaii that keep the heat and humidity from becoming oppressive. Also in the air, there must be a spirit that is evident among the family members that comes from hearing the word and keeping it, and an inner freedom born of the Spirit that dwells in each person. Joy should be more obvious in the home than the fear of sin or of doing something wrong. Likewise, there needs to be a respect for and a fidelity to the wisdom and teachings of the Catholic Church, not to mention a respect for others who do not share our Catholic faith.

In other words, taking the Catholic faith seriously means living the gospel of Jesus, that is, living in the Spirit of Jesus we received at Baptism and were anointed in at Confirmation. If we don't, then all the other things we do, even pious things, won't really matter all that much. But when we live in the Spirit of Jesus, I firmly believe that angels will be present in the details of our daily lives. Very often, my job is just to help people wake up to that wonderful truth of faith, nudging them in the direction of a way of life centered on faithful love, and not to worry.

Not too far into my initial interview with a young couple wanting to marry, I ask if they ever pray together, which is a critical first step into living a life of faith. If the future groom, let's say, is not a Catholic but a baptized Christian, it gives me an opportunity to emphasize that there is much that they have in common at a faith level and that they can share together since both believe in Jesus. It also sends a message that I respect him and his faith tradition. However, the answer I most often get to my inquiry about praying together is a somewhat embarrassed "no." By the way, I never refer to anyone as a "non Catholic." Rather than identify them by what they are not, I think it is better to identify them by their own faith background whatever it may be. If they have no faith background at all, I deal with that as best I can.

I'm sure the Catholic party is afraid I'm going to tell them to pray the Rosary every night, but I don't. Instead, I ask them if they ever imagine the day when they have a child and they will listen to its prayers at bedtime. They always nod "yes," often with a smile on their faces as they anticipate such future joys. *"That is a beautiful image to have,"* I say, but then add that as good as that is their child may grow up thinking prayer is just for little kids (and old ladies). So I take it a step further and ask, *"Wouldn't it be better to invite your child into your room at night to listen to your prayers? Or better yet, to join you in your prayers? Wouldn't that be an even more beautiful thing to imagine?"* To most young couples, this is a totally new idea, but they get what I am driving at. If the children experience mom and dad at prayer, they're more apt to "catch it."

I often tell them the story of my visit with Jack and Maxine, a couple I knew from my Marriage Encounter days. They had 17 adopted children to go with their two biological ones. They had wonderful, Christ-like hearts which they opened to take in Amer-Asian orphans who had been abandoned in places like Korea; children of mixed race, usually fathered by members of the American military stationed there. These children were often destined for the streets because no one wanted them.

When Jack and Maxine's "extended family" gathered around the huge dinner table, it looked like an assembly of the United Nations. At about 8 o'clock, the call went out that it was time for night prayers. From every corner of the house the children emerged and gathered in the living room. The prayer didn't last long, as the little ones were obviously bushed. What impressed me is that this ritual was woven into the fabric of their lives, as natural as having peanut butter and jelly sandwiches for lunch. Angels were in the details of their prayers that asked God to bless their family, friends and Freddy the frog.

As I encourage a young engaged couple to pray together, I always tell them to make it short, because if it takes too long, they won't keep doing it. Of course, they are intimidated, even fearful that their future spouse may think their prayer is stupid or something. They feel very vulnerable. Some married couples have told me that when they started to pray together they felt even more vulnerable than before sexual intimacy. So I warn the young couple about this and add, *"If the prayer is from your heart, it will be just fine. Don't worry."* What I am really trying to do is open a way for them to experience something of faith together and even to enter a bit more deeply into the flowing current of divine love that is going on between them. I don't know the long term effects of my effort, but it is always worth a try. Who knows, angels may gather around them at such times.

This does not preclude a husband's and wife's need to pray at other times, even separately. After all, the family prayer with little ones won't go deep enough to satisfy their spiritual needs as adults. But their prayer cannot be seen as one of the ten thousand things they do each day, but that practice that enables them to see those ten thousand things.[1] It helps give them a perspective on their lives and on life in general. Praying with the gospels *lectio divina* style, can be very helpful for the same reason. It enables them to see reality in a "faith enlightened" context, the way it is meant to be seen by a follower of Jesus.

When we look closely at Jesus we see that prayer was an integral part of his way of life. He often needed to get away from the crowds. Sometimes he took the disciples with him, sometimes he didn't. Through prayer, he stayed in communication with his Father. He drew strength and wisdom to address the challenges of his day. We need to do the same.

When we examine Jesus' life we also see that his love for others wasn't for show. While what he did often caused a stir, he shied away from peoples' praise. In showing his compassion for the blind, lame, possessed, sinner and outcast, he was expressing his love for them and wanted to restore their dignity and their rightful place in society. It was especially evident in the way he reached out to the sinful woman and allowed her to wash his feet then dry them with her hair. He showed it in little ways and now encourages us to do the same, like in giving a cup of water to a child. He had a special sensitivity for the oppressed, urging them to learn from him, and their souls would find rest.

In St. John's beautiful "Bread of Life Discourse" (John 6) we can almost hear the anguish of love in Jesus' voice when he turns to the Twelve and asks if they want to leave him, too. And we can imagine the sadness in his eyes when he said to Judas at the Last Supper, *"What you have to do, do quickly."* Our couples need to be familiar with the life of Jesus, because he is the one against whom they are ultimately to measure their lives of love. That is why God called them to the Sacrament of Matrimony; to show us what *"Love one another as I have loved you."* means in our world today.

A story is told of a visitor to the United States Mint where our U. S. currency is printed. He was particularly interested in that part of the tour that dealt with counterfeit money. When they got to that department, he said to the one in charge, *"You must really spend a lot of time studying counterfeit money."* *"On the contrary,"* the official responded. *"I spend all my time studying authentic bills, which enables me to recognize the counterfeit immediately."* As St. Jerome said, *"To be ignorant of the gospel is to be ignorant of Christ?"* Finding the right time of day for your quiet prayer is the challenge. It may be a little thing, but little things can make all the difference.

Speaking of little things, when I was in high school there was a popular song sung by Kitty Kallen called *"Little Things Mean A Lot."* We can't dismiss as insignificant those plain, ordinary, little things we do out of love each day. They are the very things that ultimately carry the big things. They create and sustain the atmosphere of love around moments of intimacy that give those moments their meaning. They are like the mortar that holds bricks of a cathedral together. As I recall, one verse says,

> *"Throw me a kiss from across the room.*
> *Say I look nice when I'm not.*
> *A line a day when your far away,*
> *Little things mean a lot."*

It was a simple song from a simpler age to be sure. And yes, it is probably about romantic love, but it doesn't have to be. In fact, it's often those little acts of loving sacrifice for one another in a family that most often go unnoticed that keep family members close. To me, they are evidence that the finger of God is at work in our lives. You can call it the finger of God, grace or the work of angels, it doesn't matter.

> One of our retired Irish priests loves to tell the story of the parish priest who asked Mary, an elderly parishioner, if she believed in the little people. *"Oh, gosh no, Father,"* she said. *"Well,"* the priest said, *"I understand a lot of people around here do."* "Oh, not me, Father," she assured him shaking her head. *"That is good to hear. You're sure now, Mary?"* "*Of course I don't believe in them."* Then she paused a long time, leaned toward the priest, and, as if confiding to him whispered, *"But they're there."*

* * * * * * *

Every evening at about 8:30 my father would quietly get up from his chair and leave the living room. He went to the bedroom. For the longest time I wondered why. One evening, I accidentally walked in on him. He was saying his prayers. Gosh, praying was more important that watching wrestling on television! (This was in the early 50's.) Dad is the one who took me regularly to confession. (It dawns on me now that I don't recall him ever taking my brothers.) One day he asked me, *"Tom, do you ever say the rosary?"* *"Not very often,"* I said lying through my teeth. I never said it. He simply said in reply, *"Just remember, no one will ever say it for you."* Then he dropped the subject. Some angels can be pretty blunt.

On a related issue and at a personal level, I cannot remember one Sunday growing up when my family ever missed Mass. It never happened. I can still remember when I was small sitting next to mom in church. She had an old fur coat she wore in the winter. I'd pass the time blowing patterns in it; that is, until she leaned over and said in hushed but firm tones, *"Cut that out!"* I can still remember the Mass schedule for our little, overcrowded church: 6:00, 7;15, 8:30, 9:45 and 11:00 o'clock upstairs; 9:15 and 10:30 downstairs. (Evening Mass hadn't been invented yet.) That was over 65 years ago! We never missed.

One time dad, mom, my brother Russ and I were in eastern Washington on vacation. Wheat fields stretched around us as far as the eye could see. Finally, we got to the little mission church somewhere on the way to Grand Coulee Dam just before the 9 o'clock Mass Sunday morning. The only problem was that Mass wasn't until 11 o'clock. Surely we wouldn't have to wait two hours! We waited two hours. It was a foregone conclusion for dad. Russ and I hit rocks into the wheat fields with sticks the whole time we waited. We were learning that love is faithful, but we didn't know it at the time. My three older brothers all still faithfully go to Mass each Sunday. It was in the air we breathed growing up. We caught it, or better still, it caught us. Could angels have been dodging the rocks my brother and I hit into those wheat fields? Maybe they were with dad and mom who watched us, waiting patiently together.

There was a family in my parish with six little children who came regularly to daily Mass. At least two were in diapers at any given time. I don't know how the mother did it, especially when some people tell me they are too frazzled to come to Mass on Sunday with one child. Maybe they fear embarrassment should their baby make a fuss, disturb those around them and then have to be carried out. Maybe this is why some parishes have cry-rooms. To be quiet frank, I hate cry-rooms. I detest cry-rooms! They are noisy and they stink, a combination hardly conducive to prayer.

Besides, I think that if we have a special room for crying babies, we should have a special room for coughing adults, green haired teens and old men with sleep apnea who fall asleep during my homily. Why single out parents with babies? What parent hasn't been through the experience of a fussy baby? They've all been there, so there is no need to be embarrassed. It is part of the learning-how-to-love process for parents and for members of a community. It is part of the ambience of parish life! When things get to be too much, it is easy to take the baby out. If ushers are at all on the ball, they'll help. And should an usher make the parent feel unwelcome because of the crying baby, he/she should be fired. Parishes must be family friendly. To really help young families, all parishes with small children should have a secure nursery so mom and dad can leave their little ones so they can pray the Mass together. To put this as clearly as possible, I'd rather deal with crying babies in church than the cry babies who complain about them. Now there's a group that could use a special room! (Oops! That wasn't very loving was it.)

> This reminds me of a story about a little boy who was making a big fuss during the services in a small Baptist church down south. The father finally bit the bullet, picked the kid up, threw him over his shoulder and started to pack him out. As they exited through the main door, the little guy yelled back for everyone to hear, *"Now, you all pray for me!"*

It will be a sad day when we no longer hear babies crying in our churches. Babies in a parish family are a gift. They give life. They speak of the future. I recall being at Mass in a retirement community near Phoenix. Something was wrong, and finally it dawned on me. There were no children. I'll take crying babies any day! Besides, their angels report directly to the throne of God.

Getting back to the family with the six small children, one Sunday the father was carrying his three year old son Tommy in his arms as he came up to receive Holy Communion. As I extended the Host and said, *"The Body of Christ,"* and before the father could say, *"Amen,"* little Tommy, faster than a speeding bullet, snatched the Host right out of my fingers! As he held the Sacred Host in his hand, I said to myself. *"Here goes another non-scheduled First Holy Communion."* But what he did next has made its way into my First Holy Communion homily ever since. He held the Host in his fingers, gently brought it to his lips, kissed it, and then handed it to his father. He had never heard of transubstantiation to be sure, but he had already learned that the Host was something special and worthy of respect. Faith was in the air and he was taking it in.

I tell these stories because they illustrate how the Sacrament of Matrimony most often works; subtly, without fanfare. It has a profound effect on family life and we are often not aware of it at all. That is okay, as it is a life that is not meant for show. The angels are in the details of the little things going on all day everyday – and often into the night. Let a St. Francis talk to a wolf and everyone goes agog. In the supermarket I watched a mother talk to her baby in the grocery cart, and the baby went agog, as its little arms and feet flailed excitedly. Mom cooed unintelligibly, and the baby understood everything she said. I couldn't help but marvel. Angels were in this little detail of their day together. Love was given, received and experienced. God was there. Sometimes the simplest of things can be truly profound.

This little story holds another important truth. True religion is not meant to be just in the head, an exercise of the mind. It is, above all, a matter of the heart. It doesn't have to be rational at all, although it is not meant to be irrational either. Sometimes it is trans-rational, that is, just "beyond" the rational. After all, what is rational about falling in love? In effect, to fall in love is to lose control and then to trust all will be well. For a celibate priest, it is an experience somewhat rare at best, and always difficult, as we have to stay in control and we can't leave the "all will be well" part up to chance. Yet, St. John of the Cross says that God refuses to be known except by love.[2] If I understand what he is saying, only love has the capacity to know love. Real love, not just the idea of love, has to be a part of our lives. Hence, since we are made for God, we must be made for love, all of us.

I tried to address how this can be lived out by a celibate priest in **The Celibacy Myth**, a book I co-authored with Father Charles A. Gallagher, S.J.[3] Rather than approach celibacy from the viewpoint of what it asks a priest to give up, it presents celibacy as a charism of the Holy Spirit that helps enable a priest to love his people as a way of life. It holds up the Sacrament of Matrimony as the model for the celibate way of loving. When understood, the opposite of a celibate priest is not a married priest, but a bachelor priest.

I think St. Teresa of Avila was on a similar wavelength when she said, *"It must be understood not all imaginations are by their nature capable of this meditating, all souls are capable of loving."* [4] To repeat what we said earlier, holiness must be available to everyone. It is not the privilege of the extraordinarily brilliant, learned or pious. It must be possible for the ordinary man and woman living the way of love in the context of their daily lives. It was Blessed Mother Theresa of Calcutta who said that we don't have to do great things, just small things with great love. That is in range for everyone. Moms and dads are doing it everyday, 24/7. My limited experience of people with Down syndrome has taught me that, despite their many limitations, they are people with a great capacity to love others. And ultimately, that is all that matters. I imagine their angels smiling a lot.

One summer day long ago my parents were both working in the yard, dad watering the garden and mom weeding the flowers. I noticed a strange look come over dad's face that said, *"Should I or shouldn't I?"* Well, he did. Without warning, he turned the hose on mom. Startled and feigning anger, she took out after him, threatening him within an inch of his life. The fun was on. I'd never seen that side of my parents before in my life. They were playing, having fun, and I'd guess the angels were having a good laugh. I'm sure I slept well that night. Another time, after I was ordained, we were in Germany together, dad, mom and I. We shared the same hotel room. We'd settled in for the night, and the room was pitch-black. I barely overheard my father say to mom, *"Goodnight honey."* Mom responded softly, *"Goodnight sweetheart."* It was never so obvious to me that they were lovers long before they were ever my parents. I slept well again. They were married over 59 years when mom died just before midnight News Years Eve of 1987. That night the angels wept.

I'll never forget the young man who was making a Search Weekend (teen retreat) when I was in CYO (Catholic Youth Organization) work. He was a big, husky kid, a football player. He never took off his letterman's jacket. Ten to one he slept in it. At a certain point on the weekend, the teens received letters from family members, loved ones and friends. I noticed the letterman's jacket head out the door, so I followed it. In the darkness I heard what sounded like crying. I approached the young man and asked, *"Are you okay?"* *"Yes,"* he said. *"What happened?"* I asked further. *"I received a letter from my dad and he said he loved me. I'd never heard him say that to me before."* Such a little thing. Angels were there. If fathers only knew how important they are to their children, especially their sons. If showing love is thought to be a sign of weakness, why is it so hard for some to show it? Sadly, parents occasionally refused to write to their children. At such times, angels will also be found weeping.

A young girl of eleven from our parish was diagnosed with neuroblastoma, and particularly nasty form of cancer. She was surrounded by prayer from family, friends and strangers. Her long struggle to beat the odds only ended when she exhaled her last breath. But before she did, she amazed everyone with her profound grasp of God's loving presence in her life. Somehow, she came to the mature awareness that love was all that mattered. She touched other patients in Seattle's Children's Hospital; many of whom were not Catholic, some not even Christian, who came to visit and talk with her. Her concerns were not so much about her getting well, although she wanted that very badly, but how those around her were doing. While the cancer had stripped her of her physical energy, she had another energy that seemed to blossom. Rather than surrender to despair, she surrendered to love, and it made all the difference. Rather than anger, there was a serenity about her. Angels must have been present even in her suffering, and, when the time came, I imagine them escorting her to the eternal dance of love.

The lay brother Lawrence (1611-1691) spent his life working in the kitchen of his Carmelite monastery in Paris. Surrounded by monks of great learning, he led a simple life. Yet, he wrote the following: *"The time of business does not with me differ from the time of prayer; and in the noise and clatter of my kitchen, while several persons are at the same time calling for different things, I possess God as a great tranquility as if I were upon my knees at the Blessed Sacrament."* [5]

I would hope that wives and mothers, not to mention husbands and fathers, will find in these words of a cloistered monk hope and consolation, as well as encouragement. In doing ordinary things, mundane things, even if constantly interrupted by kids underfoot, the God of love is as accessible to them where they are as he would be in the chapel of a monastery or their parish church. God is present in life, really, truly present. If we think we need to go someplace else than where we are to find God, we are truly lost. Granted, some places can be more conducive to prayer, but God is no more present there than in our kitchen.

Entering the mystery of love can at times approach the mystical. We enter an experience that is "beyond" us, one that can change the way we see life and the world. Falling in love with another person has this power. At the rookie level, scruffy looking boys start to comb their hair. But for those who are veterans, there is a longing for union, if not an abiding sense of union. We are talking about something more than physical attraction. I recall the mystic Caryll Houselander who wrote years ago about an experience she had had that was like this, but there was nothing romantic about it. As I recollect, she was just walking down a city street and suddenly became overwhelmed by seeing Christ in every passerby. It was through that experience that she realized that oneness in Christ is the only cure for human loneliness. It changed her life. She realized that *"if we only look for Christ in saints, we shall miss him."* That is hardly rational. Her arms and feet didn't flail excitedly like they did for the little baby, but the joyful emotion she felt was just as real.

Does a moment become mystical when we are overwhelmed with love? Is this what Jesus had in mind when he said, *"I want my joy to be in you and your joy to be complete"* (John 15:11)? Maybe, but I don't know if joy even has to be there. Couldn't moments of extreme sadness be mystical as well? When a loved one dies, our grief may be beyond words. Agony is something that comes from somewhere deep inside of us, and often it can only be expressed through tears and agonizing groans.

Is it possible for us to experience something of the suffering of Jesus as Mary did at the foot of the cross? If it is possible, and I'm inclined to think it is, could this not mean that we all may have had mystical experiences and didn't know it? Faith does enable us to see things differently. It may even enable us to realize that the suffering we feel may be a taste of the suffering of God within us. While humans have tried to fathom the meaning of suffering over the centuries, could it not simply be an experience that reveals to us something of the profound love of the Spirit dwelling within us? If Jesus wants us to feel his joy, why can't we also feel his suffering, a suffering born of love?

A woman came into the sacristy as I was removing my vestments after Mass. She was obviously distraught, speaking very fast, almost incoherently. It turned out that there had been a drive-by shooting and her brother was dead. She wanted me to come and administer the Last Rites of the Church. When I got there, the man's wife and young daughter joined us in the prayer. As we prayed that he was now with God, there was no doubt in my mind that God was with us. In that parking lot where evil had triumphed just moments earlier, love was now present, and in that love was our God answering the cry of the poor. Whether God was sharing in our pain or we were sharing in God's pain, I believe that in that time of shared pain born of love, angels were present. For eyes that long to see, they were there.

* * * * * * *

I think that most parish priests work pretty hard to make their parishes alive and vibrant. Most are open to any good idea that will help them in this regard. While there have been successful diocesan wide efforts with programs like RENEW, some parishes have been blessed with truly gifted pastors who used their resources well and knew how to both organize and inspire their parishioners. I heard a presentation by such a pastor from the mid-west who had worked wonders in his parish. He had groups of people trained and ready to respond to almost any need that arose; he had developed small prayer groups and mini parishes to encourage his people to come together and share faith and prayer. The music ministry was extensive and provided appropriate music for each of the various liturgies each weekend. Since his was a large suburban parish near a major city, he used his considerable resources very effectively to create a parish that could hold its own with those evangelical mega-churches that preach the "health and wealth" message as gospel.

I was exhausted just listening to him and realized that I didn't have the resources, the ability or energy to create, let alone lead, such a mega parish myself. As I reflected over the presentation, I tried to think of what was possible for smaller parishes, and those in rural areas and the inner city that were truly poor. An interesting thought came to mind. Why can't we use something that already exists in every parish that could provide the intimacy of small faith communities and prayer groups? A family is already a small faith community. Couldn't it become a prayer group? The issue wouldn't be organization, only awareness and inspiration.

Remember, when Pope Paul VI spoke of the family as the "little" or domestic church, he said that everything that could be said of the "big" church could be said of the "little" church. What if we found a way somehow to enliven our parishes around our families, or at least not ignore them? It would be affordable and even a small parish with limited resources could do it. Families could get together. Single parent families and other single people could be encouraged to join in with other families or form their own groups. Why not? It could truly increase the flow of the Spirit within a community.

My point here is simple. What we are talking about in this book is not a program. It is not something that needs someone with organizational skills or a flow chart. It is not a structure that comes down from the chancery office for implementation or needs to be included in the parish budget. When we talk about the Sacrament of Matrimony we are talking about people committed to a way of life built around the new commandment: *"Love one another as I have loved you."* It is not complicated. What a pleasant surprise!

The task of church leadership, especially the clergy, is, first of all, to help our couples understand that they have a sacred vocation from God that is crucial for the well-being and future of the church. They need to know that God has faith in them and we do, too. Our duty is to acknowledge, support and believe in our couples as living signs of Jesus' love present in the church. Our role is to empower them by believing in them, by trusting in their goodness and by respecting their extraordinary role in the life of the church: to teach us the ways of love and to make it believable. It is an awareness all members of the clergy and church leaders should have.

It just so happens that a group of married couples decided on their own to meet together following a Marriage Renewal Weekend they had attended in our parish. Whatever their agenda was each month was up to them, but they all took their marriages and their Catholic faith seriously. They invited me to attend one of their monthly gatherings, but not to give a talk or to socialize. They wanted me to hear their confessions. There were five couples and they allotted me three hours. In all my years of hearing confessions, I don't ever remember hearing any that were ever more meaningful, relaxed, serious and devout. I had to believe it was the work of the Spirit.

Obviously, these couples had come to a point in their marital relationships where they no longer expected perfection from each other. They accepted each other as is, not as they hoped or dreamed or remembered. In this extraordinary way, these couples demonstrated a way of loving each other through their desire to be better men, women, husbands, wives, dads and moms, and followers of Jesus. They face the future trying to hold together the tensions of good/evil, truth/falsehood, right/wrong, struggles/joys, life and death as the dynamic reality of their lives without criticizing each other or by getting on each other's case.

They chose to bring hope and healing to the situations of their lives. Rather than try to change each other by ripping out the weeds growing along side the wheat of their lives, they trusted the other was tending to their own garden so that they would not destroy something that they have together that is truly beautiful. Such things happen when people are open to the Spirit alive in their hearts.

Married couples living the Sacrament of Matrimony are a manifestation of the hidden mystery of God at work in their lives and in the world. They call attention to a deeper reality of the flow of divine love at work in the human heart and what happens when people choose the way of love in answer to God's call. Clearly, this is not limited to married couples, and certainly not just to Catholics, as God calls all of us to the way of love. Obviously, those who don't know Jesus can still love deeply and meaningfully. Having sacramental couples in our midst may just remind us of this wonderful truth, or they could even empower us to live the way of love more fully ourselves.

And this truth endures even when suffering enters our lives. Who willfully makes themselves more vulnerable day in and day out than a husband who loves his wife or a wife who loves her husband? Both stand to be hurt, and, eventually, it is bound to happen. In fact, this may be among the reasons some people choose not to marry at all. They'd rather "pretend marriage" than be married. They want to leave the door open so they can just get up and leave when hurt and struggle come to their relationship. I guess the idea of commitment scares them too much.

Unfortunately, the lack of commitment makes it so much easier to make that decision to walk out when problems arise. Tragically, they also end what could have been an excellent opportunity for them to mature in the ways of love and to grow as human beings. Instead, by missing that opportunity, they remain stunted in their knowledge of love, maybe even superficial. Clearly, in God's plan, commitment is crucial to any long term intimate relationship. It is not optional. It is that quality of love that opens the door to learning the ways of love when it becomes difficult. This reminds me of an old Anthony de Mello story.

One Sunday morning after church, Jesus and St. Peter went to play golf. Jesus teed off. He gave a mighty swing and sliced the ball off into the bushes beside the fairway. Just as the ball was about to stop, a rabbit darted out from behind a bush, picked the ball up in its mouth and ran with it down the fairway. Suddenly, an eagle swooped down, picked up the rabbit in its talons and flew with it toward the green. A hunter suddenly appeared, shot at the eagle and scared it enough that it dropped the rabbit onto the green. When it landed, the ball dropped out of the rabbit's mouth and rolled into the cup. Watching it all, St. Peter turned to Jesus and, obviously annoyed, said, *"Come on now! Do you want to play golf, or do you just want to fool around?"*

Commenting on this story, Father de Mello asks, *"And how about you? Do you want to understand and play the game of life or just fool around?"*

We need to remember that getting married is not just a game for the enjoyment of the couple. It is a divine institution that teaches the ways of love, even when the parties don't want to learn them. In time, however, it enables them to take their eyes off of themselves and see that life is not about them, but that they are about life. All God really wants is their hearts. When they surrender them to God, they open themselves to transformation. In turn, this enables the couple to be an instrument of transformation to the people in their lives. To finesse the hand one is dealt or to perfect a bluff won't work in the long run. It takes real commitment to love as a way of life or nothing will really change. Love and love alone has the power to transform us into people with the mind and heart of Jesus.

Walking away when things get tough doesn't help anyone. It can even do damage. I'll never forget the young woman in her mid-twenties who was considering suicide because her live-in boyfriend of three years had just walked out on her. She had surrendered everything to him with no commitments, and suddenly it was over! Living together seemed like a great idea at the time. She was confident that he would eventually marry her, not realizing that that was the furthest thing from his mind. Now she was devastated. In spite of possible warnings, the poor woman thought she had it all figured out, but learned that life was much bigger and much more complicated.

How hard it is for us to learn that life is not about us at all? We are fools to think it will adapt to us. It won't. We must adapt to it. Oh, we can get away with playing a game for a while maybe, but eventually reality gets its way. Genuine love calls for commitment and fidelity. Clearly, sacramental marriage is a threat to any arrangement based on anything else. That is why Jesus remains such a threat to anyone who chooses to live a way of life that is not based on self-giving love. That is why the church is often ridiculed for being "out of touch" with the modern world that says marriage is about self-indulgence, about "me" and "what I want." Do you remember the rich man in the gospel who had so much wealth that he decided to tear down his grain bins and build bigger ones with no thought to anyone other than himself? (Luke 12:13-21) Jesus didn't call him evil. Jesus called him a fool.

I think of the Rogers and Hammerstein words of a song from their musical **The Sound of Music**: *"Love in your heart wasn't put there to stay. Love isn't love 'til you give it away."* Life is about giving of oneself in love to another so the other can live. And the only way we can know that kind of love is to try to love the way Jesus loved. Even though we will always fall short, the fact remains that we are made for love. We are made for God. So, to follow the way of love will eventually lead to the cross. Could it be that when Jesus said, *"Unless you take up your cross and follow me you cannot be my disciple"*(Luke 14:27), it was just a variation on the theme when he said, *"Love one another as I have loved you."*

* * * * * * *

I received an emergency call to go to the hospital early one morning. It sort of irked me, really. I wanted to sleep, and where were the other priests supposedly on call? It is so easy to feel sorry for myself, so easy to think the world should adapt to me. Well, married couples are on call

24/7/365, and not just when there is an infant in the house. When their children are older, they can't get to sleep until the last one has returned home safe and sound. And let a child get sick who needs to go to the hospital, and they are there with him/her at night, all night maybe, just because they love their child so much. Of course, it could be their spouse in the hospital. They don't like spending their nights in a hospital room trying to sleep on a small cot with nurses buzzing around to take vitals every half hour, but, under the circumstances, there is no place they would rather be. *"In sickness and in health"* were words they said on their wedding day perhaps 50 years earlier, and they still live by them. These are holy people living the way of love. Why wouldn't angels be in that hospital room, too?

I've observed wives tend to every need of their husbands as they watched their strong, wonderful bodies gradually succumb to the ravages of ALS (Amyotrophic Lateral Sclerosis, known popularly as Lou Gehrig's disease). I've watched husbands struggle with the growing reality that their wives, with whom they had shared so much joy over the years, are slowly, gradually, little by little, retreating into another world while leaving the memories of this one behind as they did so. Alzheimer's is a disease that leaves both spouses alone with only one capable of feeling the loneliness of it all. But, even as I watch, I don't really know what these couples are feeling because I haven't experienced love to their depth. What makes their suffering a cross is that the loneliness and pain they feel is the end result of love. I wonder, can their angels feel it, too?

John had to wait on Aileen day and night as her diabetes had finally rendered her blind. He had built exercise equipment to help slow the crippling effects of her other ailments. She was totally dependent on him as he had to feed her, bathe her, clothe her, and care for her in everyway. They had been through a lot during their long marriage, and they were meeting this challenge like they had all the others, together.

One Sunday afternoon, John called to tell me Aileen was in the hospital and he wanted me to go visit her. When I said I would he added, *"Pick me up on the way."* When we arrived at the hospital, Aileen was unconscious. I gave her the Last Rites of the Church as John held her hand

and gently stoked her hair. On the way back home John broke the almost solemn silence by asking the question that scared him the most, *"What am I ever going to do without her?"* His words caught me off guard. What an extraordinary thing to say, I thought. She was the one who was totally dependent on him and he wondered what he was going to do without her! There is no doubt; he got it! Life was about loving others. It led to the cross, but the very love that caused the pain is the love that enabled them to carry it. It was the love of Jesus for us that made his cross different from the crosses of the two thieves on his right and left.

Granted, any misfortune or hardship is often referred to as a cross. I do it myself. But what makes the difference is love. For some people, a misfortune may lead only to a life of bitterness. That is not carrying the cross as Jesus told us. There is nothing hopeful or redemptive about it. To carry the cross is to never give up on love. For when love continues to flow through the human heart, that person's cross becomes redemptive to self and others. I think of the many severely injured young men and young women who have come home from Iraq and Afghanistan who are an inspiration to others. With love, they carry their crosses and give life. But my focus here is on those husbands and wives who suffer the crosses that inevitably come their way because of their love for God, each other and their families. To me, they are heroes too, and an inspiration.

This is to say, we don't have to go to the celebrity, the hermit, the contemplative, the canonized saints of the church to find truly holy people. If we have eyes to see, they are all around us, many looking like ordinary husbands and wives, fathers and mothers, sons and daughters. Like Jesus, many of them are victims, who never play the role of a victim and never create other victims. They say, *"Father, forgive them for they know not what they do."* Others, and rightly so, are compelled to end tragedies like sexual abuse by bringing it to light, or the destructive behavior of an alcoholic spouse by seeking intervention. While some have become bitter, most continue to let love guide them.

But most holy couples I know are just busy with the demands of ordinary life. They are hard at work trying to heal wounds, to raise their families, to deal with the job or the lack of job; to pay the bills, and make ends meet; to care for a sick child or an aging parent, and through it all to remain faithful in love for those in their lives. The vast majority of married couples I know bring love to bear on the issues of their lives, as that is their *modus operandi*, their way of life.

* * * * * * *

When I first came to St. Vincent de Paul Parish, I looked out over the congregation at Mass and saw missalettes looking back at me. So, preferring to see peoples' faces, I got rid of the missalettes except for those who truly needed them, the hard of hearing. In time, as I looked out, I could put names with the faces. After a few years, I looked out over the people and saw stories. A parish is made up of individual stories, some joyful and some sad; some about life and some about death; some tragic enough to make you wonder what life is all about, and others so wonderful that all you can do is to stand in awe and say thanks.

But those individual stories formed another story, "our story," that is, the story of St. Vincent de Paul Parish. Each person and each family touched other individuals and families; we formed and shaped one another as we carried on the work of the parish, be it during the sacred liturgy, while teaching in a religious education program, when preparing Thanksgiving baskets for the needy, or when having fun on a sunny day during the fall festival. We celebrated with each other when our children got married, prayed together when our children were stricken with illness, and consoled the mourning when loved ones died. We tried to be there for one another as we realized that our Catholic faith was not about "me" but "us." We were a part of something bigger than ourselves and we liked it. We even felt better about ourselves and our identity as Catholics. As a parish community we turned outward toward our larger community to help those in need, our other brothers and sisters, spiritual relatives, distant cousins and total strangers in the spirit of our patron, St. Vincent de Paul. They were a part of our story, too, but our story didn't end there.

As a parish, we knew that we were also a part of "The Story" if you will. God invited us into the world of grace, into the divine story of love that existed for all eternity. Taking the initiative, God shared with us the gift of divine life. Our parish was a "graced reality" as God was a part of our lives and we were a part of God's. Like "my Story" and "our story" the history of the "God-with-us story" was one of joys and sorrows, hopes and disappointments, hurts and healings. But above all, it was the story of love lived out in the context of the human experience, and since "where love is God is," God was living with us in our communal and individual stories. And from our experience of "The Story," we began to learn that love alone could satisfy the human heart and its deepest longings. And because we were a part of The Story, our story was also a story of hope, for while there were other things that now and then happened that tried to sidetrack the human spirit, it somehow always found a way to come back to its center, love.

We further discovered that it was The Story that gave ultimate meaning to "our story" and even "my story." Rather than smother either of them, it enhanced them and gave them purpose. It confirmed the idea that life is ultimately about love, and our giving of ourselves to others in love so they could live. And when we lived that way, we found fulfillment, for we were living our dignity as children of God and respecting that same dignity in others. And right at the center of "The Story" was the human family. I think we could even say that *"as goes the family, so goes the church."* And at the center of the family was that sacramental couple trying to enflesh in their lives the new commandment, *"Love one another as I have loved you."*

Among the many wonders of the sacred liturgy of Eucharist is the fact that it is there that these three stories merge. We come as individuals to gather in community because we were invited by Jesus to "eat and drink." Standing at the altar *in persona ecclesiae*, the priest raises his arms for the concluding doxology of the Eucharistic Prayer, the sacred hosts in his left hand and the chalice with the precious blood in his right. And as he sings, *"Through him, with him and in him ..."* he is offering himself and the people as they are at that very moment to the Father in union with Jesus. It is the most significant of the three elevations at Mass, as it is at that moment that we, priest and people together, surrender ourselves to that Love we call God the Father who, at that moment, is loving us.

I like to imagine that in my extended left hand offering the hosts are all the one, true, good and beautiful things about us; our joys and victories, our happy times, hopes and moments of peace and times of loving intimacy experienced since our last sharing of Eucharist together. And in my extended right hand offering the precious blood are all of our sorrows, pains, worries, anxieties, failings and doubts that we have experienced since our last time together. We offer ourselves as we are, saints and sinners, in union with one another and in union with Jesus to the Father. By this liturgical action, we surrender ourselves with Jesus to the Father as he leads us more fully into the eternal dance of divine love so that the spirit of that dance will enter more fully into us. And, bit by bit, with each Holy Communion we receive, that divine love will transform us and our hearts more into the likeness of Jesus.

In many ways, the Eucharist celebrates the very pulse of life with all of its joys and sorrows, victories and defeats, hopes and concerns. And most amazingly, we don't just offer Jesus to the Father, but we offer ourselves as individuals and as husbands and wives, brothers and sisters united to one another and with Jesus to the Father. That is to say, we offer the Church, the Body of Christ to the Father. This means that the Jesus we offer is the Jesus who exists today, united to us, living among us, who shares all of our joys and sorrows with us. Through the Holy Spirit, Jesus is a part of our lives at every moment of everyday, and tangibly so, when we are living the way of love. He said he would be with us always, and I believe him enough to take him at his word. In fact, I've staked my life on it.

Furthermore, it is that Eucharist that constantly reminds me that life is not about me at all, but that I am about life in Jesus. And that life in Jesus happens whenever two or three of us gather in his name, whenever and wherever it may be. It is then that I realize that Jesus is calling me to surrender myself to the Father in love, for it is in that surrendering that I find life. I think of how our sacramental couples model this kind of surrender to each other day after day throughout their long years of marriage. The irony of it all is astounding. We think we go to Mass to get something, but are empowered, instead, to surrender something, to abandon ourselves to God, and then, to top if off completely, are commissioned to show that same kind of loving, surrendering behavior to the people in our lives. And really, I don't know who does this more credibly on a regular basis than our sacramental couples living their extraordinary vocation of love day after day.

While we are all called to live the commandment of love in its depth, it is the presence of our married couples in our midst who call us by their lives to do so; who show us The Way, who teach us the fundamental mindset of the Christian life. Our sacramental couples need to be aware of this and how crucial they are to the life of the church. It is for them, above all, that I set out to write this book. Others could have done it better, but it needed to be said. Now our task is to believe in our couples, to thank them, and to support them in every way we can. After all, they got married, not just for themselves, but also for us! May our good God bless their love for each other, and through them, continue to bless us. Truly, they are precious gems in the mosaic of our lives. Or, as we are saying here, they are a pearl of great price, worthy of our gratitude and deserving of our faith.

CONVERSATION STARTERS:

1. When have you experienced "angels" in the details of your life?

2. What has helped your prayer life as individuals and/or as couples?

3. In matters of your faith practices, what is non-negotiable?

4. Was Jesus more divine during the Transfiguration or when in the Garden of Gethsemane? What's the point of this question?

5. Would you recommend coming to Mass as a family? Why?

---

1. See Richard Rohr, O.F.M., Everything Belongs, (New York: The Crossroad Publishing Company, 1999) p. 93

2. bid., p. 95

3. Gallagher, Vandenberg, *The Celibacy Myth*, (Crossroad Publishing, New York, NY 1987)

4. Noteworthy, Quotations from Collected Works of St. Teresa of Avila; Institute of Carmelite Studies, Washington, D.C. ICS Publications; Book of Foundations, 1982

5. Robert Ellsberg, All Saints (Crossroads Publishing, New York, 2007) p.24

APPENDIX A:

Pastoral Concerns

1. Contraception

When we talk about the importance of sexual intimacy in marriage, we have to admit there is something of an elephant in the living room of most Catholic homes. Of course, not many of us really want to talk about it, but it's there. I'm referring to the whole issue of artificial birth control. Should the issue of marital sex come up in Catholic gatherings, the conversation usually dances around the subject. If we had to bet on whether or not our friends, parents or kids are practicing or have practiced contraception, the odds would tell us to lay our money down on the square marked "Yes." But, of course, we choose not to go near that table because who wants to get into that discussion among friends and family? They've probably made up their minds already, and that's that.

There are some who think we priests should preach about it more, while others wish the whole subject would just go away. I haven't heard any evidence that Pope John Paul II, who frequently addressed the issue in his visits to the United States, changed peoples' minds to any significant degree, let alone behavior. I doubt if I could either. Perhaps I could help some people feel a bit more comfortable in knowing that I am loyal to church teaching, and help others feel more guilty, and thus get them to reevaluate their behavior, maybe even change it, but I'm not so sure it would make things much better.

A number of things come into play when I consider this issue. For starters, the last thing I want to do is to needlessly alienate anyone. I compare it to giving someone a blood transfusion. The guy may need one, but if I give him the wrong type, it could kill him. So we need to be careful. I think it is safe to say that the majority of Catholic couples of childbearing age practice birth control of some sort at one time or other with no apparent qualms. I even received a note once from a mother telling me with much joy that her son had just had a vasectomy. So it doesn't take a genius to deduce that countless couples with small families probably planned it that way. They aren't all just lucky at love rhythm style. They practice birth control. According to one report, Catholic couples "quietly ignore" teachings with which they disagree and that Catholic couples use birth control regularly (Murphy/Banerjee, New York Times, 4/11/09). While I understand that morality is not determined by popular vote, the prevalence of using artificial means of contraception cannot be ignored. Just what this says is open for debate, with many saying that the church lacks credibility in this area. It's an argument I choose not to go into here. So what do I do? How do I handle this issue pastorally? So, for what it's worth . . .

When a couple comes to me for counsel in this area, I always explain the church's teaching on contraception. I present it as clearly and as positively as I can. I don't criticize it, belittle it nor argue with it. It's not my place to do so. I want to faithfully and responsibly represent the church and its values in this regard. I must be careful not to disregard it as silly or old fashioned, or be condescending in any way to those who faithfully follow it. I've seen arrogance on both sides of this issue, and that does look silly.

In the back of my mind is the awareness that our culture seems to be almost anti-child, and even discourages couples from having children. Not only does it warn that raising children is terribly expensive but also that it will interfere with your lifestyle as adults. In short, social pressure discourages many couples from having children altogether, let alone more children. If, however, a couple simply lack a desire to have more children, I may encourage them to pray for that desire as that might be the only thing stopping them. But I hesitate to push them into having more children. In either case, I encourage them to reevaluate their situation as time goes by since conditions change. Having another child just might be the best thing that could happen to them.

In all honesty and in fact, we priests don't fully grasp what a couple may be going through. It is one thing to talk to a couple when both are active Catholics who want to do everything the church teaches, but quite another when one party in the marriage is a lukewarm Catholic or is of another faith, or of no faith at all. When the issue of artificial birth control comes up (They may be practicing it already.), I help them distinguish between those methods on the market that simply impede conception from those that are really forms of abortion, like the morning after pill and IUD's. They are quite different. I make it clear that any method that may contribute to an abortion is gravely immoral and therefore seriously objectionable and can never to be used.

But what do I say to couples who have several children and clearly want to follow the church's teaching but feel trapped? Those who come to me for guidance have always been couples who practice their faith and would accept another child without hesitation if they conceived one, but judge that they are not in a position to have one at this time. The issue could be the health of the wife, the finances of the family, or just the conclusion that their family is big enough. It's a judgment that I have to respect. And the reason they have come to me is often because of the tension building between the husband and wife around their sexual relationship. Being open to the conception of new life could also be stifling the quality of openness and joy in their relationship. Fear, anxiety, guilt, anger and confusion may all come into play and gradually become a wedge between the two. I recall talking to an older woman who said she felt abandoned by the church when she was in her 40's. With five children already, the church left her and her husband to fend for themselves as their priest simply restated the church's official teaching on artificial birth control. She admitted to feelings of alienation at the time.

If the couple has not attended a course on Natural Family Planning, I strongly urge that they do so, and give them a contact to call. I tell them that it will help them understand not only how NFP works but that when understood, it may well be the best solution for them and I encourage them to try it. I also add that it will also help them share the responsibility for their sexual relationship. Sharing this responsibility is always important, but especially so at times of tension between the couple. It will also help them appreciate more fully the physiology of their bodies and the wonder of this important dimension of their lives together. Few realize that when NFP is faithfully followed, it has a 99% success rate, about the same as the pill. Recommending NFP may be all I need to say.[1]

I am also very careful not to put down or make fun of Natural Family Planning as it is the only clear avenue of birth control that our couples have that has 100% official approval by the church (aside from abstinence of course). Furthermore, I respect greatly our couples who are committed to it or are willing to try it. I know many couples struggle with this decision and I don't want to discourage them in any way. I also know that in these relationships there can still be fears of another pregnancy which may cause one or both parties to feel reluctance and/or guilt around intimacy issues. As a group, these good couples can also really feel abandoned by some in the church, so I feel especially protective toward them. We all struggle to follow the way of Jesus, which is not easy for any of us. Should a baby come unexpectedly, I always make it a point to rejoice with the couple at the good news. Maybe that is just my way of saying thanks to them for their deep faith and their extraordinary openness to life.

Occasionally, the couple "*has been there done that.*" Now what do I say? Well, I never give them permission to practice artificial birth control. It is not my decision to make, nor a permission I have the authority to grant. Nor do I simply dismiss their concern by glibly saying something like "*Oh, that's up to you,*" like it doesn't make any difference. It does make a difference, a big difference! They come to me for help, and I want to help them; to reassure their goodness as they face this real dilemma. Some may think that even considering some form of artificial birth control is a sin, when in fact, it may be arising out of their basic goodness and sense of responsibility.

And so I try to explain to them the concept of "tension morality." It happens when two Catholic values come in conflict with each other. For example, the church teaches that artificial birth control is wrong. When a couple decides it would not be wise for them to have another child and they still have strong sexual desires for each other, well, that causes tension #1. Tension #2 comes from the church's teaching on responsible parenthood. That is to say, couples must act responsibly in raising their children. This is certainly implied when the church says that matrimony *"is by its nature ordered toward <u>the good of the spouses</u> and the procreation <u>and education</u> of offspring."*[2]

Education is both formal and informal, with much informal learning coming from the atmosphere present in the home. One very significant influence on the spirit in the home is the quality of the sexual relationship being experienced by both husband and wife. When the couple's sexual relationship is free of tension, there is often a peace and joy between the couple that affects the spirit in the home. And this joy adds a dimension of credibility to whatever they try to teach in matters of faith. As I like to say, *"Faith is more often caught than taught."* But when tension exists between the couple over their sexual relationship, that tension can overflow into the home, fill the air, and often render the gospel of love harder to hear.

This second tension could mean that a couple may not think that having another child is a good idea at this particular time, possibly for health or financial reasons. However, they must use care lest they use these as excuses rather than reasons. (My folks had good reasons not to have a fourth child during the Great Depression; but fortunately, they found a good enough excuse to have me.) While some suggest that God will take care of them no matter what, I find it hard to urge that as a solution to their problem even if I believed it myself. I can't impose my faith on them and thereby expect them to follow something they don't actually believe themselves. Should one party decide to trust God and the other is resistant to that trust, I may actually have made things worse.

Furthermore, when we factor in the awareness that the Sacrament of Matrimony isn't just for the couple themselves but for the church, it should heighten their realization that the quality of their relationship will have a real, if not profound influence on others, especially their children. As indicated, the kind of atmosphere present in the home is not to be taken lightly. Couples have shared with me that the health of their relationship can also affect their performance at work and interaction with others in general. Should a couple grow distant from each other, more anxious and less trusting, it can eventually have a negative effect not only on the couple's marriage, but also on their whole family, not to mention on their friends and co-workers. Therefore, I certainly don't want to stifle the flow of the Spirit between them, as it is crucial to the quality of their relationship. And, of course, they want to keep their relationship with God healthy as well.

So now there are two teachings of the church in tension with each other: no artificial birth control and the call to responsible parenthood. What does a couple do? I tell them that they need to pray about it first and ask for the guidance of divine wisdom. We can't forget the role of God's grace at work in their hearts. And then I say they need to make a choice one way or the other, as many good, holy and responsible couples have before them, a choice they can both own. And that is pretty much where I leave it. As I said, it's up to the couple to make that decision, not me. What I need to do is respect their conscience which they have tried to form responsibly.[3]

This approach will not be acceptable with everyone. Some will reject it outright, especially if they cannot get past the idea that every act of sexual intercourse between a husband and wife must be open to the conception of a new human life, and that's okay. It is our church's teaching. But there are other couples who can't get past the idea that they, as responsible parents, have a strong, moral obligation to weigh the pro's and con's and then do what their good judgment tells them.

Do such couples feel regrets when they judge that such a decision is the best decision for them under the circumstances? Yes, I'm sure they do, at least that is my understanding. But they are in good faith, and I appreciate how they can come to make that decision. In an ideal world, they wouldn't have to, but they don't live in an ideal world. As mentioned earlier, I encourage them to reevaluate their decision down the road should their family situation change. Life is messy, but if they have the desire to please God in all they do, that desire pleases God.

We priests must be sensitive to the difficulty many of our couples face, and respectfully honor their decision. They need to sense that we support them in their desire to live holy lives. Regardless of what their decision is, both sets of couples believe that sexual intimacy must be open to new life, although one does not restrict "new life" to conceiving a baby. It is also seen as embracing the well-being of the family, not to mention the health of their own relationship.

While I have a concern that a couple may ignore the negative consequences another child could have on them and their family, I'm also concerned for the couple who may ignore the negative consequences that the decision not to have more children could have on that couple's relationship and their family. If a couple isn't careful, their sexual intimacy could become just an empty action void of any real meaning. Since there would be no real anxiety about conceiving a child, sexual activity could become just that, an activity, not an act of self-giving love for one's spouse. I fear that that has happened all too often to the detriment of many couple's relationships, thus bringing significant harm to them and to their families, not to mention society. Some have separated sexual intimacy from the generation of new life altogether, and once that is done, sadly, the meaning of sexual intimacy is susceptible to forms of distortion beyond all recognition. We see it all around us today.

Artificial birth control is not a silver bullet that will solve all marital problems. To the contrary, it could also give rise to new problems, including such things as the possible harmful side effects of using certain medications. There are claims and counter claims about the link between taking the birth control pill and some forms of cancer. I would advise any couple, Catholic and otherwise, to check this out carefully and responsibly. If I were them, I would want to know how these medications work, what they do to the body, and the risks involved. After all, if the pill tricks the woman's body into thinking it is pregnant, what other tricks might it have up its sleeve? More could be at stake than we think. This whole issue is evidence that life is not easy. That is why the couple's commitment to

Jesus and to the way of love is the most critical decision they can make. Let's not ignore the importance of prayer and the need for divine guidance.

In this matter, we priests have to be conscientious about what we say. We can be right or we can be wrong. We can be too dogmatic or too lax. We need to pray for divine guidance, too. What is important is the condition of the hearts of those who come to us. I assume their good will. Yet, we can't help but react to the stories we hear. We feel pain when we see dreams die, as I did with that young mother I mentioned earlier whose husband had the drinking problem. But our couples who come to us want help. To give it, we must be humble enough to admit our need for wisdom from above. And that wisdom can only exist in the atmosphere of love.

---

1. NFP is most difficult during a woman's fertile time. Ron and Cathy Feher address this issue in the "Living In Love" program suite developed and promoted by The Pastoral and Matrimonial Renewal Center, P.O. Box 2304, Southeastern, PA. 19399. *(www.lovinginlove.org.)*

2 . Catechism of the Catholic Church, New York: An Image Book, 1995), #1601

3.   Gaudium et Spes, Vatican Council II, #16

2. Same Sex Marriage

Marriage is much bigger than we are. It is not just about the couple who marry, or their personal happiness, as though it were a private affair just between the two of them. Whether they like it or not, the way they live together will have a profound impact on the lives of others, and not just their children. And that will have a profound effect on society. It is a truth we simply cannot afford to ignore. That is why society, for centuries, has had a stake in marriage. This is even true among aboriginal peoples. There are expectations placed on the couple relationship by the society in which it exists for the good of that society.

The nature of the marital relationship, while it arose from the physical, emotional and psychological makeup of the man and the woman to meet their needs, also met the needs of society. It set certain standards for marriage because it needed marriage to be strong for the well being of the community; it wanted to help strengthen and support it in order to foster good social order, especially around the generation of new life and the raising of children so they would grow up to be responsible members of that community. While the marriage was clearly a relationship between a husband and wife, it always had implications for the well being of the society in which it existed and for its future.

This extended relationship of the couple to the larger community is evidenced by the civil requirements for a valid marriage. It was never about just the couple in isolation from the larger reality of society. An obvious example would be laws forbidding marriage between couples who were first cousins. While, over the centuries, there was an evolution of the expectations of the society on the couple relationship, it was always between a man and a woman with an eye toward the future. There are many at work in our society today who are mustering all the pressure they can to change this.

I really hesitate to get into this issue as it is so complicated, so political, so fraught with emotion and so polarizing. But it needs to be addressed as it will profoundly alter the way we look at marriage. And that "new look" will have a profound effect upon our society. I'm speaking of the major effort in our culture to call the domestic partner relationship between persons of the same sex "marriage." But I'll take a swing at it in terms of what we are trying to say in this book.

By way of background, let us begin with the definition of marriage as expressed in the Catechism of the Catholic Church which unambiguously states the vision of the church.

> *"The marital covenant, by which a man and a woman establish between themselves a partnership of the whole of life, is by its nature ordered toward the good of the spouses and the procreation and education of offspring; this covenant between baptized persons has been raised by Christ the Lord to the dignity of a sacrament."* (#1601)

Interestingly, this definition of marriage has been challenged by many outside the Catholic Church long before the concept of same-sex marriages ever arose. To be specific:

- We call marriage a covenant, while many see it only as a contract. Rather than being based on a love relationship, it is based on justice. (Think prenuptial agreements.)

- Marriage is intended for the *"whole of life."* That means that by its nature marriage is intended to be indissoluble, that is to say, the bond of marriage is unbreakable. Divorce and remarriage is not allowed. (This is a complicated issue, but the nature of marriage calls for permanence.)

- The *"procreation and education of offspring"* is simply ignored by many couples who could but have no intention of having children in their marriage. Should a couple of childbearing age marry with the deliberate intention of never being open to children, even if both are not Catholic and the wedding takes place in a secular setting, the marriage would be seen as invalid by the Catholic Church.

- The idea that marriage was raised to the *"dignity of a sacrament"* by Christ the Lord is simply not believed in many Christian communities.

So, the Catholic Church has a long tradition of proclaiming marriage as it sees it even though it is unacceptable to many. The idea that marriage is of its nature to be between a man and a woman is just the latest thing to be challenged. While the church is not indifferent to civil law surrounding these other issues, it has found a way to live compatibly with them.

But the issue of same sex marriage is different and more perilous. It not only takes exception to a religious understanding of marriage, it now disagrees with the traditional civil understanding of marriage enough to want to redefine it, that is, to make marriage itself something it has never been before, a union of persons of the same sex. Whichever way this issue is resolved in our country, it will have no effect on Catholic teaching, but that does not mean it will not have a negative effect upon society-at-large and also the church. In fact, it will. So, reluctantly, here are my thoughts.

In my opinion, the concept of marriage will be reduced in terms of its meaning to describe any legalized relationship between two people who love each other, or whatever. The campaign to call such a same sex relationship "marriage" is an attempt to legitimize it in the eyes of society by putting it on a par with the traditional marriage relationship. To be sure, the current weak state of marriage in our society has provided an atmosphere that has contributed to this. Behind the pressure for same sex marriage is the underlying factor that traditional marriage in our culture is seen to be disintegrating, and with it, the family unit. Of course, they go together. I will get to that in a moment.

The arguments for and against same-sex marriage are many, and I don't want to get into all of those here. But from what I have been saying in this book, the reason that speaks to me as clearly as any of the others comes from the fact that there is nothing intrinsic to same-sex marriage that speaks to anything beyond the relationship of the couple. Aside from what happens to the couple themselves in terms of legitimizing their relationship, nothing else is asked or expected that is not present in a committed domestic partnership. That cannot be said of a heterosexual couple who marry. When I was in high school, I recall seeing a newlywed's car with tin cans tied to the back bumper and the words *"Watch Burien Grow!"* written on the trunk. The obvious implication was a rather crude way of saying that their marriage was expected to have an effect on society, especially in terms of children.

When a man and a woman marry and thus commit to a sexual relationship, they have to address a question that may never cross the mind of same-sex couples: *"Do we want children?"* The very nature of man/woman sexual intimacy forces them to look to the future and what the future might bring in terms of a family. It forces them to look outside of themselves because they can see that their marriage is not just about them, but also about children that they may bring into the world. It is a reality that arises from the intrinsic nature of their relationship as a heterosexual couple. And they have to answer it with either a *"yes," "no," "not now"* or possibly *"Let's see what happens."*

The moral theologian Philip S. Keane, S.S. makes the following relevant observation.

> *"It is the conjugal union of the couple that makes possible all the values at stake in marriage. The man/woman relationship which is so meaningful in life as a whole is most deeply realized by the personal union of the spouses in marriage. The physical intimacy, which is a universal human need, is most fully able to be realized through the union of spouses in marriage. Children are the supreme, concrete manifestation of the physical, personal, and social union of the spouses. But marriage is still marriage even when there are no children, (e.g., in cases of sterility). And unless children spring from the kind of total and permanent union of spouses just described, the life situation of the children will be sadly lacking. Thus, it seems essential that we declare the union of the spouses in*

their otherness to be the focal point from which marriage is to be understood both humanly and Christianly. If we too quickly move to the children in defining marriage, values essential to marriage and to the children may be lost sight of." [1]

The reality is that when we speak of same-sex marriage we will not have to mention or think of children at all. They will have become irrelevant to the institution of marriage entirely. In the effort to be "fair" to gay and lesbian couples by redefining marriage to include them, it seems we may well have done something that could become, in time, very unfair to children.   When children are ignored, the consequences can be devastating, as revealed in a cover article in <u>TIME</u> magazine. It highlighted the social tragedy and the negative effects the breakdown of marriage is already having on children, not to mention society in general.

There is no other single force causing as much measurable hardship and human misery in this country as the collapse of marriage. It hurts children, it reduces mothers' financial security, and it has landed with particular devastation on those who can bear it least; the nation's underclass. ... The growing tendency of the poor to have children before marriage... is a catastrophic approach to life. ... Children from intact, two parent families out perform those from single parent households. Longevity, drug abuse, school performance and dropout rates, teen pregnancy, criminal behavior and incarceration – if you can measure it, a sociologist has; and in all cases, the kids living with both parents drastically outperform the others. ... Few things hamper a child as much as not having a father at home. The feminist sociologist, Maria Kefalas, said, "Women always tell me, 'I can be a mother and a father to my child,' but it isn't true." Growing up without a father has a deep psychological effect on a child. "Mom may not need that man," Kefalas says, "but her children do." ... Princeton sociologist, Sara McLanahan, adds,

"Children growing up in a household with only one biological parent are worse off, on average, than children who grow up in a household with both of their biological parents, regardless of the parents' race or educational background."... It is dismissive of the human experience to suggest that kids don't suffer extraordinarily from divorce. Then, David Blankenhorn, president of the Institute of American Values observes, *"Children have a primal need to know who they are, to love and be loved by the two people whose physical union brought them here. To lose that connection, that sense of identity, is to experience a wound that no child-support check or fancy school can ever heal."...*The article concludes with this observation. *What is the purpose of marriage? Is it ... simply an institution that has the capacity to increase the pleasure of the adults who enter it? If so, we might as well hold the wake now: there probably aren't many people whose idea of 24-hour-a-day good times consists of being yoked to the same romantic partner, through bouts of stomach flu and depression, financial setbacks and emotional upsets, until after many a long decade, one or the other eventually dies in the harness.* [2]

Clearly, the collateral damage of the sexual revolution has been and continues to be very costly. We are paying a great price in human suffering as a result of it. Playing fast and loose with Mother Nature has indeed proven to be a very dangerous thing to do.

Yet, and sadly, to speak openly in favor only of heterosexual marriage does not go with the flow of what is deemed politically correct. And to object to same-sex marriage is often to be labeled as homophobic. So, unless there is somehow a true renewal of marriage in our society, the church will be seen more and more just an "out-of-date" voice crying in the wilderness, probably bigoted to boot. This is grossly unfair.

Since the nature of same-sex relationships does not and cannot fit the traditional understanding of marriage - which always included the procreation of children - it demands that the definition of marriage be changed to fit it. And with that change of definition our culture will be ignoring totally the traditional, crucial and unique place marriage has had in society, especially as that place best suited for bringing children into the world and giving them a healthy start in life. (You might want to reread the observation of David Blankenhorn above.)

This does not mean that kids can't be raised by single parents or in broken households or even by gay couples. But countless studies, reinforced by the TIME's article, have shown that the stable family of a father and mother is best suited for the healthy raising of children. In effect, should single-sex marriage become the law of the land, our culture would be saying that there is no longer a specific institution in our society that is distinctively constructed or intended for the procreation and raising of children. After all, if marriage is just a private right between two people, with no social responsibilities that flow from the nature of the relationship, it makes sense. But its consequences make for chaos.

Sadly, according to a 2007 report, 40% of all children born in the United States were born to unwed mothers.[3] This number grew from 20% in 1980 and 26% in 2002. I have heard that it is currently at 47%. As one observer said, *"Marriage isn't viewed anymore as central to rearing children."* We shouldn't see that as a good thing, especially for the kids. Yet, that is exactly what we are saying when we advocate same-sex marriage. Rather than affirm marriage as irrelevant regarding children, we should be working for its renewal in society.

I've tried to be open to the reasons why same-sex marriage is a good idea, but I keep running into realities that trump those reasons every time. Clearly, what Blankenhorn says above about children's need to love and be loved by the two people who conceived them is one of them. But there is more. When society says two men or two women can marry each other, it makes the issue of children and how they come into the world irrelevant. Do we as a civilized society really want to say, *"Hey, everyone, have your kids any way you want, it doesn't matter?"* Sorry, but it does matter, again, especially to the children. It's either that or we are saying kids themselves don't matter. But kids keep coming, and that fact is exerting tremendous pressure on social service agencies. Also, as we said earlier, when sexual intimacy has been totally separated from the whole issue of creating new life, all kinds of distortions of sexual behavior enter the picture. One can't help but wonder if same sex marriage would legitimize them as well.

Being opposed to gay marriage has nothing to do with the need to support all efforts to protect gays and lesbians from true discrimination and to give them social safeguards so they are free to live as they wish. While many people have serious reservations about the gay life-style, I don't hear anyone really arguing against the idea of domestic partnership. To be against same-sex marriage is not discrimination. It is only facing into the reality that marriage means something that is crucial to the well being of our society that gay and lesbian couples are incapable of meeting. Sexual intimacy has profound consequences for a husband and wife that go far beyond their personal desire and sexual satisfaction. It is not just about them. When a child is conceived, it changes their lives forever. It is a dimension of marriage that a gay couple never has to face. However, should same-sex marriage become law, that which is unique to heterosexual marriage, and is so significant for millions of heterosexual couples, will be ignored by society as irrelevant. And that would be a major blow to the special place marriage has in society.

When you change the definition of marriage, your aim is to change the way people will look at and regard marriage. Marriage is something wonderful and sacred, so why would we even want to change it? What does same-sex marriage add to the concept of marriage? If anything, it takes meaning away. Is this really what we want to do? Granted, marriage is in a sad state, but do we really want to throw out the baby with the bathwater, literally? A definition is meant to identify a reality in truth. So, to redefine marriage to accommodate couples who are obviously incapable of fulfilling one of its most fundamental purposes makes no sense. It is an attempt to re-form marriage around the couple, rather than have the couple reform their lives within the marriage.

Let's take it to another level. I'll never experience the feelings a mother has when holding her newborn. But what if that's my desire? Shouldn't I have a right to be a mother? What difference does it make if I am a man? Why don't we just redefine a mother as anyone who holds a newborn? Why not? Well, besides being really absurd, it devalues the intimacy, the tenderness, the awesomeness of the mother-child bond, and the wonderful fact that the newborn is the incarnation of the love that exists between her and her husband, the baby's father. The child is the fruit of their love for each other.

I asked a mother recently as she held her four week old daughter if she ever thought of her baby as the love between her and her husband made flesh. *"Oh yes,"* she said. *"We are in awe by what has happened to us. We talk about it at night. It has brought us so much closer."* Her husband enabled her to become a mother. She enabled him to become a father. Same sex couples can never have that same conversation because their reality is fundamentally different. To pretend otherwise is also absurd.

No matter how we define "mother," I'll never be one. I can't be. I'm a man after all. To say anyone can be a mother is ridiculous, because everyone can't, even if they want to. Equality and fairness have nothing to do with it. Similarly, in saying that of its nature, marriage is *for the procreation and the raising of children*, it necessarily embraces all that goes with that emotionally, physically, psychologically and spiritually. In a gay marriage, it just isn't the same. It can't be. Among countless other things, gay couples have different expectations, hopes and dreams. To call their relationship "marriage" defies common sense.

The one thing you will never hear gay couples say to each other is *"I am carrying your baby."* Should they have a child, it was not conceived by a sexual act of self-giving love of one spouse to the other. Parenthood, by design, would no longer be a grace of matrimony, but a "grace" of in vitro fertilization, artificial insemination or surrogate motherhood. By design, the baby's biological father or its biological mother will not be an intimate part of its life.

In same sex relationships, the love that is meant to be present in the act of a child's creation will not be there to surround it when that child is growing up. The child, by design, cannot love the two who brought it into existence. Again, this is not criticizing the need for children to be adopted so they can have a chance at life, but I get nervous when we start creating babies to be adopted. Something is wrong. Adoption has always been a Plan B arrangement for the well-being of the child first, not to meet the needs of couples who want children.

> A teacher asks her students, *"If you call the tail of a dog a leg, how many legs does the dog have?" "Five?"* a child guesses. *"No,"* the teacher says, *"It only has four. To call a tail a leg doesn't make it so."*

What makes this issue so difficult is that the Catholics I know support society's efforts to embrace our brothers and sisters in the gay community so they can live full, productive and peaceful lives. If laws need to change to insure that this happens, we are behind those changes. We have children, brothers and sisters, relatives and friends who are gay, and love them no less for that fact. They are a part of our lives, and we hurt with them whenever we hear they are treated with hatred and discrimination. I asked a friend that left the priestly ministry who eventually entered a committed gay relationship what he thought of gay-marriage. He said that another name had to be found because marriage already had a specific meaning that is important for married couples and for society.

It seems to me that a right is not a true right when it is exercised or enforced at the expense of someone else's right. (Unfortunately, our society has already violated this principle when it says a woman has a right to choose an abortion at the expense of her child's right to life.) Also, there would not be any need for the tremendous social pressure, even intimidation, to advance the cause of same-sex marriage if it made sense in people's minds. Married couples deserve to have their marital relationship respected for what it is and a right to have that marriage protected and supported as necessary for the future wellbeing of society. But, sadly, in our present culture, there are no guarantees.

Having said all this, the temptation for some in the church may be to simply write off gay couples. I don't know how we can do that. I personally think there is much to be learned that we do not know about this whole issue and what it means than to simply say, *"This is what the church teaches, too bad."* We must look for ways to minister to those of our communities who are gay or lesbian, not to mention the whole array of "gender alternatives" out there. There should also be some way for the church to tap into the richness of their lives as well, as there is much they can offer us to help us be a healthier community of faith and a better society.

I have no question that God loves them all. That is never the issue. To even raise the question is to project onto God our own prejudices. The issue is how does the church show its love? What does that love look like? Unfortunately, the issue has been so politicized that real love may be incapable of being recognized anyway. Rather than closing the book on the issue by edict, I'm inclined to hope we are just opening it up.

———————————————————

1. Philip S. Keane, S.S., *"Sexual Morality - A Catholic Perspective,"* Pualist Press, New York/Ramsey/Toronto, June 1, 1977, p. 93

2. Caitlan Flanagan, *"Why Marriage Matters,"* TIME Magazine, 13 July 2009

3. The Seattle Times, 14 May 2009; from a study by the National Center of Health Statistics

3. Cohabitation

What about couples who come to get married who are already living together? Much has been written about this from many angles, so my observations will again be around the running theme of this book, that marriage is a social sacrament in, of and for the church. For what it is worth, it is the pastoral approach I use in this difficult situation. Quite simply, marriage of its nature, sacramental and otherwise, is social in nature. It is for the benefit of society. Cohabitation, on the other hand, is for the couple only. I don't expect it will strike a chord with everyone, but I do hope it will encourage priests to be truly pastoral in their approach as well.

For me, the real tragedy of this living arrangement is that it is often made up of two people who may well be enamored with the notion of their personal independence. What others think about their living together isn't of major concern to them, and if it is, they want to exert their independence anyway. True, their parents may object, but it is their life and what can parents, or anyone else for that matter, do about it? It's a free country, so it is their choice and no one can really stop them, not even the church because they can always get married somewhere. But they think, for whatever reason, that a wedding in the church would be nice; so why not?

What the couple cannot see is that what they so admire in each other, their independence, could be the very thing that will eventually begin the unraveling of their marriage. They are used to the idea that the world adapts to them, first as individuals and then to them as a couple. There is a certain social isolation going on, especially with their families. Their parents love them dearly, but feeling powerless, they are often hesitant to talk about the cohabitation situation, hoping a wedding will come sooner rather than later. Of course, to counter this parental reticence is the support the couple receives from friends who are doing the same thing and from our culture that glorifies independence and simply accepts cohabitation as being part of the modern culture. Unbeknownst to the guy, the gal often sees cohabitation as part of the natural evolution leading to marriage, while he sees it just for what it is, cohabitation, with marriage no where on his radar. Yet, if such concerns are expressed to them by clergy, they are dismissed as misguided or just old fashioned. After all, they are young and up to date, caught up in the ways of the modern world. Yes, that may be true, but while times change, human nature doesn't.

After awhile, those things they admired in each other, like their individuality and independence, start rubbing the wrong way in a marriage, and while she wonders why he doesn't go along with her plans, he wonders why she doesn't go along with his. They begin to realize that the one they married doesn't treat them as the center of the universe, and that they cannot count on getting their own way all the time. If they are not careful, that old stubbornness they so admired in each other morphs into selfishness. When that happens, the honeymoon is over!

They never realized that the human relationships that last are those that place the other before oneself, and that being a husband is all about the wife, and being a wife is all about the husband. Unfortunately, living for someone else has not been their pattern of life. Therefore, while such rude awakenings are common to all marriages, they are especially troublesome for those with a mindset of independence that says, *"No one is going to tell me what to do."*

What is worse, it may be harder for a cohabitating couple to hear the message of sacramental marriage; that it is not just for them, but also for the people of the church, a church that may have become irrelevant to their lives. And since they may have also drifted from the practice of their faith, it is a message they may not be interested in hearing anyway. Of course, that could be true of other couples as well.

So, when a couple comes to me, I want to know if they are living together, not to make a moral judgment against them, to shame them, or even to try to correct them, but to guide what happens in my meeting with them. I ask them flat out, *"Are you living together?"* If they answer yes, I say with a fair amount of disappointment in my voice, *"I am so sorry to hear that."* Often they'll stiffen a bit preparing their defense, but I don't argue with them about it at all, and they can't argue with my feelings of disappointment which are real. Then I add, *"You didn't expect me to be in favor of your living together, did you?"* *"No,"* they reply. *"Good,"* I say, *"We have just settled the morality of it, at least according to the teaching of the church. You know it is wrong."* Realizing what just happened they know they can't plead ignorance.

It is at this point that I just talk to them, asking why they want to get married in the Catholic Church. If one is not a Catholic, I express my gratitude to them for being willing to be married in the church of their future spouse. This gives me a little leverage to encourage a lazy Catholic to return to the practice of his/her faith. I take my time, being as sensitive and as loving as I can be toward them. (And I keep canon law discretely out of sight like that bedpan.) I let them know that I am aware of the pressures in our secular culture that encourage their living together, and the peer pressure that comes from their friends. But then I try to give them a vision of sacramental marriage and how it is so much bigger than the two of them. Very often, it is something they just hadn't given any thought to. I remind them that they'll learn this in a big hurry should they be blessed with children.

I have found that they are usually quite receptive to this broader vision of marriage, even the party who isn't a Catholic. I always tell them that we'll do everything to help them have a beautiful wedding, but that our real goal is to help them have a great marriage. In this context, I lay out our pre-marriage program. I let them know that I am on their side in that I want the best for them. But I also let them know that there won't be any magic come their wedding day. So I encourage the Catholic party (parties) to come to Mass and prepare their hearts for their marriage by returning to the sacraments when they can, beginning with confession. I remind than that their partner respects their faith enough to get married in their church. *"So live it,"* I say. I also challenge them to consider living apart till their wedding, or at least to stop sleeping in the same bed. While I tell them that I will not take the role of a policeman, I also ask them to discuss and pray about it. On occasion, one party will actually move out or the couple may choose to sleep in separate rooms, or so I have been told. I choose to believe them.

> This reminds me of the time Paddy was going to confession and the priest asked him, *"Paddy, have you ever slept with a woman?"* After a long and reflective pause Paddy answered, *"Well, I suppose I dozed off once or twice."*

Even though the couple chooses to stay together and make no effort to adapt their lifestyle, I don't threaten them by refusing to have their wedding unless they straighten up their act, as it were, since they have a right to marry in the church. But I do explain why having a nuptial Mass would be inappropriate, and then encourage a simple ceremony without Eucharist. I want to give them a positive experience with their wedding and wedding preparation, as it could be our last chance to reach them. To my surprise, it is often the one who is not Catholic who seems most appreciative of my efforts. I try to plant seeds. That's all I can do. I hope the soil is receptive. If so, I trust God's loving grace will do the rest. It may produce a yield that is thirty, sixty or a hundredfold. Sometimes it has.

I also keep in mind that they will be expected to attend our six week marriage preparation program when they will have further opportunity to address and discuss what it means to be married in the Catholic Church. Realizing that it probably took a good deal of courage to approach the church for their wedding in the first place, I don't want to play into their fears by making the experience unnecessarily difficult for them. Rather than take an adversarial role, I let them know I am on their side, as I mentioned already, and want the very best for them. Again, if we don't love people the way they are, we don't love them at all. If we let love guide what we choose to do, my guess is we will do no harm, and that's something. Who knows, we might even do much good.

APPENDIX B

Poems

Over the years, St. Vincent de Paul Parish has tried to support our married couples by showing them that we believed in them and by thanking them for their commitment to love each other *"for better or for worse."* That was the purpose of our annual "Lovers Celebration" around Valentines Day. It always began with a special Mass, followed by a dinner/dance in the parish hall. During the homily time, I'd talk to the couples more than preach to them, often telling stories that related to marriage in some way, like the story of John and Aileen which I've included in this book. After a few years, I could repeat some of my favorites for the newcomers who hadn't heard them, like the time Bob told me how he and his wife of over 50 years ended up with six children. They'd be in bed after a long day and he would lean toward her and ask, *"Do you want to go to sleep or what?"* And she'd say, *"What?"*

I wrote the following poems for these special evenings. I played some nice background music as I read them, making them sound better than they actually were, but the couples seemed to enjoy them. The third poem was written about three recent events that had happened in the parish and were fresh in everyone's mind. I include them here for what they are worth hoping you will read them and find something worthwhile for your life's story. (I recommend that you play some soft background music at the same time. It may help.)

THIS MATTER OF THE HEART

Where does it start, this matter of the heart?
  What's the genesis of this life-source called love?
    Although we can fake it, it's clear we didn't make it.
      It could only have come from above.

When the first man was lonely, he thought ... *"If only,*
  I had someone to share life with."
    So he did what was smart, he abandoned his heart;
      To his God, the source of his myth.

When the transformation was through, the man at last knew,
    He needn't even be lonely again.
      Standing by his side, was the prototype bride,
        Co-sharing a mysterious, awesome power from within.

In a spirit of elation, they would continue the creation,
  Of the world in keeping with God's plan;
    When everything was fresh, this two in one flesh,
      Modeled God's unity, the basic vocation for woman with man.

We are born with it still, this remarkable power to fill,
    The life of another with love,
      So we look and search, even if it means going to church,
        For that someone to share life with, hand-in-glove.

But the process takes heart, for it's really an art;
    This searching for a partner in life.
      We can't place our reliance, on the wonders of science,
        It can't tell us what makes a good husband or wife.

The subtle way to measure, this kind of treasure,
　　Is to listen for inspired promptings from within.
　　　　If from the moment you met her, you began feeling better,
　　　　　　About life, maybe something big was about to begin.

If he's handsome, use care, question his self-confident air.
　　They're no assurance to marital bliss.
　　　　Whether he's sensitive and kind, keeping you in mind,
　　　　　　Is far more important than some hot, heavy kiss.

While it may take only a shove, to enter the dance of love,
　　Living it requires much more to be sure.
　　　　While she may be a good looker, or even a good cooker,
　　　　　　They're no guarantee her love has the power to endure.

So watch out for pretense, or the dangerous nonsense,
　　That says lasting marriage is predestined by heavenly mirth.
　　　　It comes in a kit, that you erect bit by bit,
　　　　　　In the everyday struggles down here on earth.

Wives, we cherish the day, your father gave you away,
　　Proudly escorting you down the long aisle.
　　　　And the faith you displayed, as the processional played.
　　　　　　I've never seen a bride without grace, beauty and style.

And we have to make room for the oft-forgotten groom,
　　Who waits patiently, like rehearsing for a new way of life.
　　　　But what does he care, *"She's coming, right there!*
　　　　　　In just a few minutes, she'll be my wife."

To celebrate their union, they share Holy Communion,
　　By drinking of the one cup from above.
　　　　They are united as one, in the Spirit of God's Son,
　　　　　　Committed to a life of self-giving love.

Whatever will come, they pledge to meet as one,
    Fearing nothing as they stand strong together.
        It's best they don't know, where life's path will go,
           For ahead is all kinds of weather.

So they begin their life's dance, in the spirit of romance,
    Discovering little things they never suspected.
        "Listen to her snore!" "You left your shorts on the floor!"
        Such irritating things, they never expected!

Only God's wisdom could fashion, the genius of passion,
    To carry them over their little tiffs and blunders;
        But their love grew, and gradually they knew,
           The force between them could actually work wonders.

Only love that is real, has this wonderful power to heal,
    And the capacity to keep a maturing relationship fresh.
        And it is the key to God's plan, for woman and man,
           When Divine Providence ordains their love become flesh.

They never imagined the joy, at the news, *"It's a boy!"*
    Or the thrill of holding their new baby girl.
        Grandparents go wild, at the birth of the child,
           Who is more precious than any diamond or pearl.

But before they get set, their baby takes a step.
    "She's about to do it; now everyone hush!"
        But the greatest joy of all, happens down the hall,
           When she learns how to go potty and flush.

And what's this I hear, some sobs and a tear?
    Isn't this the liberation for which Mom prayed?
        But it happens at school, like by some unwritten rule,
           When her baby enters the First Grade.

Looking back it's a blur, to the things kids had to endure,
    In the process of just growing up.
        From running in races, to being fitted for braces,
            In discovering girls really wouldn't make them throw up.

Kids begin with three, and advance to two.
    (The wheel, that is, invented in times of yore.)
        But all parents say, what makes them turn gray,
            Is when their teen wants four, with five on the floor.

Slumber parties weren't bad, or trick-or-treating without Dad.
    Insignificant, but passages still.
        But it went by so fast, would the important things last,
            Like the values you tried to instill?

First Communion was more, than a time to adore,
    Little girls and boys in full dress.
        Would they recall, after they had grown tall,
            God was with them, to guide and to bless?

When kids are naive, it's easy for them to believe,
    But you can't protect them from the world's deceit.
        Will God's truth they had studied, become all muddied,
            Or still nourish and remain ever sweet?

When parents were young, fear often tempered their fun,
    As veterans, it's still much the same as before.
        Their feelings are mixed, as they stand there transfixed,
            Watching their 6 foot 2 "little one" stride out the door.

Maybe it's off to college, to gain significant knowledge,
    The fulfillment of careful planning to be sure.
        Or maybe it's just moving out, to check what's about,
            It's a child's passage all parents must endure.

It's like giving birth, but this time without mirth,
    Their genuine happiness too overwhelmed to show.
        There's no child to hold, and they're tempted to feel old,
            As their treasured memories surface and overflow.

It's often shocking what's left, after the birds leave the nest,
    "What's happened to our noisy, hectic house?"
        "The place seems so quiet, like it's on some pointless diet,
            The music just doesn't sound right. It's Strauss."

And then you rediscover, your partner as lover,
    For years disguised as baby-sitter, chauffeur and nurse.
        You forgot she was yours, not just a doer of chores,
            You took her for granted, and possibly even worse.

You lost sight of your dream, or so it would seem,
    When you complained that he was married to his job.
        He hated to shop, and seldom took time to stop,
            As you begged him to fix that thing-a-ma-bob.

At last, you're receptive, as you regain your perspective,
    Of a life that centers on each other as it should.
        You don't need a sleuth, to dig out the revealing truth,
            You entered the Sacrament of Matrimony, not parenthood.

Now you're back to where it starts, this matter of the heart,
    That creates homes and families and such.
        The power that brings life, between a husband and wife,
            May need nothing more than a soft, gentle touch.

As the years sail along, like the tempo of a song,
    Their dance moves from Rock to Western to Waltz.
        But to think lasting love slows, when the hearing goes,
            Is to draw a conclusion that's tragically false.

Not clear what it meant, that they were a Sacrament,
 At least not in the fancy words a theologian would say,
  Yet, they believed their love, was somehow touched from above,
  And God used them to embrace his world each day.

And then before long, love sings its most painful song,
 When one partner loses a piece of their heart.
  Having fulfilled their dream, their commitment supreme,
  In faithful love, when death does them part.

There is no way to measure, by money or treasure,
 The riches that such a shared life can sew.
  Love is stronger than fear, that's the message I hear,
   And the most precious gift anyone, anywhere, could know.

Like the first man who was lonely, the widowed says, *"If only,*
 I had my sweetheart still by my side."
  But patiently they endure, trusting their heart's longing for sure,
   Believing they will be one again, in God's love, side by side.

So that's where it starts, this matter of the heart.
 It could only have come from above.
  It ends where it starts, in the gracious flow of God's heart.
  As they joyfully share in the eternal dance of Divine Love.

       Lovers' Celebration 1991

THE LOVE BETWEEN YOU

It is time we honor what goes on between you,
     Not you as bride,
          Nor you as groom,
               Not even you as husband and wife,
               Not you at all.

We honor your love,
     Which comes, in part, from each of you;
          Your gift to each other,
               That creates you anew.

We take this time to honor the sacred,
     The love between you,
          That is nothing less than a sign
               Of God's love made visible,
                    For all the world to see;
                         And in the seeing,
                              To be drawn into the ways of love.

It is between you
     That God's power does its creative work;
          Not in the man alone,
               Nor in the woman by herself,
                    But in that wonderful space between you,
                         That you fill with your love.

Love must be between you,
     Or there is nothing between you.
          Only emptiness,
               And your marriage is a wasteland.

But when love is between you,
　Your differences are blessed,
　　Opposites attract,
　　　Creation continues,
　　　　And God says, *"It is very good!"*

When love is between you,
　The meaning of a sunset changes,
　　As does the meaning of a meal,
　　　A song,
　　　　A glance,
　　　　　A touch.

Even the atmosphere in a room changes,
　Children can feel it,
　　It has warmth,
　　　The blush of joy,
　　　　A feeling of security.

When love is between you,
　You have a channel to see clearly
　　The beauty of the other,
　　　The stupidity of clinging to a hurt,
　　　　The foolishness of refusing to listen,
　　　　The wisdom of forgiving.

When love is between you,
　You understand the wise man who said,
　　"God will hold us accountable
　　　for every pleasure
　　　　that is not enjoyed."

When love is between you,
  You continue to create the beauty of your spouse,
    And begin to wonder deep in your heart,
      How beautiful God must be
        Who first created her and molded him
          In the Divine Image.

When love is between you,
  You take time to notice,
    You take time to say it,
      You take time to remember it.
        You take time . . . to be.

When love is between you,
  You recall the wall hanging that says,
    "Peace is seeing a beautiful sunset ... and knowing who to thank,"
      As your love invites you to look beyond its beauty
        To the Mystery it makes real.

When love is between you,
  The intensity of your desire
    Unites the physical with the spiritual,
      The sensual with the mystical,
        The human with the divine.

When love is between you,
  Your two stories become one,
    Your distinctiveness makes room for union,
      And you are in awe by the wonder of it all.

When love is between you,
  There is no room for manipulation,
    No place for self-seeking,
      And no need for worry.

You become aware that life is a gift,
 That creation is unfinished,
  And that, somehow, God trusts you
  To help finish it
   With your love.

When love is between you,
 You look at yourself in the mirror,
  And may doubt your worthiness;
   You may question your readiness,
    You may wonder what you know,
     Knowing only that you love,
      And trust it is enough.

When love is between you,
 You are caught up in a mystery,
  Not to be solved,
   But to be lived.

You see how wonderful life really is,
 And you hold on to it,
  You taste it,
   You savor it as on your tongue,
    Lest it slip away too fast.

When love is between you,
 You dread the day it will come to an end,
  For something this wonderful
   Couldn't last forever,
    Could it?

Then you remember:
  God is Love!
    Where love is, God is!
      Love never ends!
        Love is stronger than death!
          Even for a man and a woman.

When love is between you,
  The goal of your journey together
    Is no more important
      Than the journey you share,
        Day by day,
          Week by week,
            Year by year,

. . . When love is between you.

Lovers' Celebration 2001

SOME THINGS ABOUT LOVE . . .

It's all about love, our life on this earth.
 That's why God made us, and brought us to birth.
  To learn how to love is the greatest human quest.
   For without a loving heart, we can't be our best.

It begins in the womb, thanks to our dear mother's choice,
 We first heard about love from the sound of her voice.
  You see, the journey is one we can't make alone.
   Life demands other people even after we're grown.

The lessons of love are as natural as laughter,
 They come at us from everywhere, faster and faster.
  From holding Dad's hand on the way to the store,
   To holding my sweetheart's while we walk the shore.

Such learning about love is fun and filled with desire.
 And from the new knowledge we gain, we never seem to tire.
  But there are other things about love, out there as well.
   And the stories behind them are never easy to tell.

The journey of life is unpredictable at best,
 And when the unexpected happens, it's almost impossible to
 digest.
  There are some things about love we don't want to learn,
   But, sooner or later, it will be our turn.

There is no way to escape it, no where to run;
 We have to stand there and face it, until it is done.
  We are tempted to blame, or in anger ask, "Why?"
   But we are powerless before it, as hard as we try.

A child is born, our hearts fill with glee,
    Is it a him? No, it's a she!
        But the doctor then tells us something is wrong,
            And the joy immediately drains from our song.

In the midst of our pain, our worry and fear,
    Our love finds expression in the form of a tear.
        There are some things about love we don't want to learn,
            But, sooner or later, it will be our turn.

Our son is now grown, successful and healthy,
    He's doing quite well, but still short of wealthy.
        Then something happens, from out of the blue,
            Maybe it's nothing, just a form of the flu.

But something is growing that's not supposed to be there.
    While doctors all huddle, we turn to prayer.
        When the surgery finally comes, we anxiously wait,
            Hoping against hope we're not too late.

Our love is so strong, and God's presence is near.
    But deep inside lingers the cold ache of fear.
        There are some things about love we don't want to learn,
            But, sooner or later, it will be our turn.

They raised all their kids, at last they're now free,
    So it's off down the highway to see what's to see.
        But before they get far, Mom gives us a start;
            At the hospital we discover it involves her heart.

A judgment comes down, like from the high court,
    It says Mom's rich and full life may now be cut short.
        She rallies, her mere presence gives us a lift.
            Then, suddenly, it's over, as she surrenders life's gift.

We gather together as family; friends, parishioners, the children and Dad.
   Who'd ever thought love could feel so lonely and sad.
      There are some things about love we don't want to learn,
         But, sooner or later, it will be our turn.

The story is told a thousand times over, and more.
   We know that someday, it will come to our door.
      We want love to be happy and joyful and sweet,
         But Providence ordains that life just isn't that neat.

Sometimes life is broken, and wounded, and filled with much grief.
   But we can't settle for just finding relief.
      There's something to be gained there, in the midst of it all.
         Because learning how to love is the heart of our call.

How precious it is, this life that we share.
   Our love for each other, knowing in times of need each will be there.
      The mystery of Divine Providence that lets evil transpire,
         Also gives us the incredible power to love and inspire.

We are born to love, what else can I say?
   From what Jesus told us, there is no other way.
      Yes, there are some things about love we don't want to learn,
         So that's why God gave us one another, when it becomes our turn.

Lovers' Celebration 1997

6422623R00120

Made in the USA
San Bernardino, CA
13 December 2013